LIFE AFTER SLEEP
THE ADVENTURES OF
A LUCID DREAMER

by

Michael E. Morgan

LIFE AFTER SLEEP

THE ADVENTURES OF A LUCID DREAMER

Copyright © 2023 by Michael E. Morgan

All rights reserved. No part of this book may be reproduced or transmitted in any form or by any means now known or to be invented, electronic or mechanical, including photocopying, recording, or by any information storage and retrieval system without written permission from the author or publisher, except for the inclusion of brief quotations in a review.

For information write to:
Dawntrader Books, LLC
34522 N Scottsdale Road
Ste. D120-413
Scottsdale, Arizona 85266

If you are unable to order this book from your local bookseller, or Amazon.com, you may order directly from the publisher.
Quantity discounts for organizations are available.

Cover and book design by
Michael E. Morgan

Publisher's Cataloging-in-Publication Data
ISBN 9-780990-313-35-9
10 9 8 7 6 5 4 3 2 1

Table of Contents

Introduction..4

Chapter 1: What are Dreams..................................22
Chapter 2: What is Lucidity....................................27
Chapter 3: Subtle Body vs Physical Body.......................32
Chapter 4: The Astral Body...................................38
Chapter 5: The Silver Cord...................................42
Chapter 6: The Astral Kingdom..............................47
Chapter 7: What is Consciousness...........................50
Chapter 8: Dreams and Time..................................55
Chapter 9: What is an OBE....................................59
Chapter 10: Preparing for an OBE............................62
Chapter 11: Time Travel and Remote Viewing..............70
Chapter 12: Two Levels of the Astral Field..................76
Chapter 13: Techniques for Lucidity.........................79
Chapter 14: Point to Point vs Real Time Travel.............81
Chapter 15: The Problem of Adolescence....................83
Chapter 16: The Illusion of Death............................87
Chapter 17: States of Extraordinary Consciousness........91
Chapter 18: The Kundalini Spiritual Practice................94
Chapter 19: Adventures with Astral Traveling..............99
Chapter 20: Contacting Another Person....................111
Chapter 21: Bilocation..115

Epilogue...120

Bibliography..132

Introduction

The importance of dreams goes back to ancient Sumerian cuneiform clay tablets, which showed some evidence of dream interpretation dating back to 3100 BC. In the history of Mesopotamia, dreams were important. Looking into the future through dream interpretation was of keen interest and popular amongst many of the Kings.

For example, Gudea, the king of the city-state of Lagash, (reigned c. 2144–2124 BC), rebuilt the temple of Ningirsu because of his dream.

In the epic of Gilgamesh, there are many accounts of prophetic dreams. In two of his dreams, Gilgamesh first sees Enkidu, then he sees an axe fall from the sky while people gather to admire and worship him. Gilgamesh throws the axe in front of his mother, Ninsun, and grasps it. Ninsun then interprets this image as a sign that someone powerful is going to appear to him.

Gilgamesh fights with the powerful one to overpower him, but he fails. Then eventually, he becomes friends and they accomplish many great things together.

Dreams can also enter another world. They

Introduction

believed that the soul moved out of the body and could visit places and people while sleeping. In the Sumerian tablet VII, Enkidu tells Gilgamesh that he saw the gods Anu, Enlil, and Shamash condemn him to death. Enkidu also dreamt of visiting the underworld. Later in the epic, Enkidu dreams about an encounter with a giant Humbaba.

The Assyrian king Ashurnasirpal II (reigned c. 883 - 859 BC) built a temple to Mamu, possibly the god of dreams, at Imgur-Enlil near Kalhu. Later, the Assyrian king Ashurbanipal (reigned c. 668 - 627 BC) dreamt during a military offensive of his divine patron, the goddess Ishtar. She appeared promising that she would lead him to victory.

The Babylonians and Assyrians divided their dreams into "good and bad." The gods sent the "good" dreams, and demons sent the "bad" dreams. We have discovered collections of dream omens entitled Iskar-Zaqiqu which record dream sequences and prognostications of what will happen to a person in each dream based on prior cases, listing different outcomes, based on people that experienced similar dreams and different results.

Dream sequences included daily work events, journeys to different locations, family matters, encounters with human individuals, animals, and deities.

The Greeks built temples for healing they called Asklepions. People got sent to be cured at these healing temples. They believed they could accomplish cures through divine grace through healing dreams within the temple. They also considered dreams prophetic as omens of particular significance.

In the 2nd century AD, Artemidorus of Daldis wrote a text called the 'Oneirocritica' (The Interpretation of Dreams). Artemidorus believed dreams could predict the future. He defined many approaches to dreams. He felt the use of the word cyphers could resolve the meaning of a dream image. They could understand by deciphering the image into component words. As an example, Alexander, during the war against the Tyrians, dreamt a satyr danced on his shield.

Artemidorus reported that Alexander's dream meant Satyr equals sa tyros ("Tyre will be thine"), predicting Alexander's military success.

During the middle ages, medieval Islamic psychology suggested certain hadiths showed dreams comprised three parts. Early Muslim teachers believed there were three kinds of dreams: false, pathogenic(to cause a disease) and true.

Ibn Sirin (c. 654–728) famous for his book on dreams called Ta'Bir al-Ru'ya and Muntahab al-Kalam fi Tabir al-Ahlam. It divided his text into twenty-five sections on interpretation, including the etiquette of interpretation and interpreting reciting certain Surahs of the Qur'an for a dream. Ibn also wrote that it was important for the layperson to seek the advice from an alim (Muslim scholar). The scholar would guide the interpretation of the best understanding of the dream context culturally and for other causes.

Ibn Sirin spoke about a man who saw himself giving a sermon from the mimbar: "He will achieve authority and if he is not from the people who have any kind of authority, it means that they will crucify him."

In his consciousness studies, Al–Farabi

(c. 872 - 951) wrote about the cause of dreams, appearing in his 'Book of Opinions' about the people of an ideal city. He was the first to define the difference between dream interpretation and the nature and causes of dreams.

Ibn Khaldun Muqaddimah (c. 1377) stated that "confused dreams" are "pictures of imagination which are stored inside by the perceiver. Then understood only when the ability to think applied after the 'man' has retired from his sense perception.

Ibn Shaheen stated: "Interpretations change their foundations according to the different conditions of the seer of the vision, so seeing handcuffs during sleep is unpleasant, but if a righteous person sees them, it means stopping the hand from evil."

In the sixteenth century, a standard traditional Chinese book on dream-interpretation contained high principles of dream interpretation, written by Chen Shiyuan. Like other Chinese thinkers, he raised the question of how we know we are dreaming and how we know we are awake.

In the writings of the Chuang-tsu: "Once Chuang

Chou dreamt that he was a butterfly and while as a butterfly he knew nothing about being Chang Chou. When he awoke, he found he was still Chuang Chou again. He wondered now, did Chou dream that he was a butterfly or was the butterfly dreaming that it was Chuang Chou?" This raises the question about reality monitoring in dreams, an intense topic of interest in modern cognitive neuroscience.

In the seventeenth century, the English physician Sir Thomas Browne wrote about dream interpretation. Dream interpretation by this time became an important part of psychoanalysis. By the end of the nineteenth century, the perceived content of a dream revealed its latent meaning to the psyche of the dreamer.

In 1900, Doctor Sigmund Freud wrote extensively about dream interpretation as part of his psychoanalytic work. His book was called 'The interpretation of Dreams.'

They endorsed this Freudian viewpoint of dreaming more significantly than the theories of dreaming attributing content to memory consolidation, problem solving, and or random brain activity. Freud's idea led people to the importance of dream content rather than thought content while awake.

Freud argued in his book on interpretation, the motivation of all dream content was wish fulfillment. Later in his book, 'Beyond the Pleasure Principle', he discusses dreams that did not appear to be from wish fulfillment. Often the origination of a dream was from the events of the day preceding the dream. Freud called this "day residue." Freud claimed with children, they dream straightforwardly of wish fulfillment aroused by the previous day's experiences. In adults, however, distorted dreams are a heavily disguised derivative of latent dream-thoughts present in the unconscious. The dream conceals the real significance. He stated, "Dreamers are no more capable of recognizing the actual meaning of their dreams than hysterics can understand the connection to and significance of their neurotic symptoms."

Carl Jung did not dismiss Freud's model, but believed his view of dream interpretation limited.

Freud's procedure of collecting associations to a dream would bring insight into the dreamer's mental complex. A person's associations to anything could also reveal the mental complexes which Jung had shown experimentally, though he felt associations would not bring one closer to the meaning of a dream.

Jung felt that dream interpretation was larger, reflecting a richness and complexity of the entire unconscious. Jung believed the psyche to be a self-regulating organism where conscious attitudes are likely compensated for unconsciously within the dream by opposites. He believed dreams could lead the person to wholeness through "a dialogue between the ego and the self." This dialogue would include fresh memories, existing obstacles, and future solutions. Later, Jung developed a theory about mass consciousness where the subconscious of all people got connected. He called this idea "collective unconscious" and suggested there was a shared foundation for the profiling of mass consciousness and beliefs beyond the individual.

In 2009 Carey Morewedge and Michael Norton

wrote a paper for the Journal of Personality and Social Psychology, where they said most people believe their dreams reveal meaningful hidden truths. A study conducted in the United States, South Korea and India found 74% of Indians, 65% of South Koreans and 56% of Americans believe their dream content carried meaningful insight into their beliefs and desires. For example, Americans were likely to miss their flight if they dreamt of their plane crashing on the night before. Studies found people would perceive their dream content more meaningful if the content fell into accordance with their beliefs and desires during wakefulness.

Reaching for and accessing the unconscious realm must have its roots in the understanding the human nervous system. The autonomic nervous system is part of the peripheral nervous system. It regulates the involuntary physiological processes, which include heart rate, blood pressure, respiration, digestion, and the libido.

There are three anatomically distinct components: the sympathetic, the parasympathetic, and the enteric. The sympathetic and parasympathetic nervous system has both sensory inputs and motor outputs to the central nervous system. The enteric nervous system is a webbed structure which contains 100 million neurons with over 15 morphologies and is chiefly responsible for the digestive processes.

In the decade of the 70s, a neurological analysis of the pathways of the neocortex of certain yogis monitored during their meditative state revealed the control of some of these autonomic functions directly. Adapting a variation of the yogic meditative approach offered the average layperson trained in the changed technique, the opportunity to accomplish the same results in the short term without many years of yogic training. This process was called biofeedback.

The target response sought after with biofeedback was to control heart rate for stress reduction and the control of blood pressure to support cardiovascular issues. The subject would be told to listen to an audible tone of a particular frequency. By lowering the tone, the indirect reaction with the autonomic response was to lower the rate of the heart and or the blood pressure. This was a very useful technique affording some people who could accomplish this mental technique, to eliminate the need for medicines to accomplish this same control chemically.

Because the effects were random and not always successful, and depended on the individual's ability to concentrate to accomplish this feat of mind control over the body, made the technique sort of faddish and unpopular within the mainstream of the masses.

Then, in the early 80s, a fresh approach developed from the concepts of Anthony Buzan regarding the idea of the brain being bifurcated, having two hemispheres functioning with the five senses working in a compartmentalized fashion. Tony suggested they might use a way to synchronize the two hemispheres to function synergistically as one mind and one brain. With this idea, he suggested the promise of raising the cognitive function of the brain from less than ten percent to greater than fifty percent nominally. They scoffed his suggestion at and disregarded as idealistic fantasy.

Introduction

In mainstream science, neuroscientists analyzed the brain's natural frequency and tagged certain frequencies to various moods that arise due to stress and or emotional swings in a response to the environment.

There are four distinct mood states that correspond to four distinct frequencies. These are: Beta, Alpha, Theta and Delta. They correspond to 15 - 30 hertz, 7-15 hertz, 4-7 Hertz and 1-4 hertz, respectively.

It characterizes the Beta state by the activity of the normal waking state, which may range from 15 to 25 hertz depending on the stress level experienced during activity, with 30 hertz being the high stress level and 20 Hertz being at a normal level.

The Alpha state is that condition just before the head hits the pillow, a relaxed near sleep state that can range anywhere from 15 hertz down to 7 Hertz, with the higher frequency nearing the awake state and the lower frequency approaching a deeper sleep state. The Alpha state is the condition needed by the body to heal itself during sleep. They also attributed this range to the condition of 'rapid eye movement', or REM, respective to the activity of dreaming.

The 'ah-ha' moment of solving a problem characterizes the Theta state and can range between 7 Hertz down to 4 hertz, with 4 hertz reflecting a state of meditation or deep concentration.

The Delta state is a deeper sleep condition usually arising after 4-5 hours of deep sleep. The actual purpose of this level is unknown. Many neuroscientists strongly conjectured its purpose, all with different opinions. Though these frequencies are present on the head at anyone time, the predominate frequency seems to follow the above criteria.

Some scientists at Columbia university, inspired by Buzan's theories, happened on the idea of creating a 'pilot tone' that would indirectly influence the hemispheres in the brain to track a desired target frequency recognized as the brain's own frequency. To accomplish this feat, a technique of feeding the mind two different audio tones one into each ear, but each tone would be below the threshold of normal hearing which means the audible level of the tones had to be less than 3 decibels (below the threshold of conscious hearing). This was to prevent the mind from isolating the disturbance of the dissonance and shutting down or discriminating against the tones all together from the hearing.

The dissonance is when two tones occur simultaneously. In this example, a tone of 30 hertz heard on the left side while another tone of 20 hertz heard on the right side. The mind is a natural organizer and is constantly looking for ways to simplify all incoming data, whether it be audible or visual, into neatly packed quanta. As the mind tries to resolve the dissonance, it mixes the two tones together, internally creating a 'pilot tone' or beat tone of 10 hertz. This mixing is called heterodyning.

Similarly, radio transmissions use this technique. The frequency of the carrier needs to be very high in order to transmit many frequencies over a narrow band, allowing many radio stations to broadcast their signals at closely packed frequencies in a band and. The voice is at a very low frequency by comparison, such as 3 thousand hertz as compared to 100 million hertz. To resolve a voice from a carrier frequency, they add the voice to a mid-frequency. Then that mid-frequency alters by mixing the voice together. Then the two frequencies piggyback onto the higher carrier frequency by modulating either by Amplitude Modulation (AM), or by Frequency Modulation(FM). The radio receiver end also has within its circuitry the same mid-frequency. When receiving the carrier, it mixes the local mid-frequency and the carrier frequency together. The difference between the two is the voice or music that is heard.

Now, in the brain's case, when resolving the difference or beat frequency internally, the mind takes that frequency, the 10 hertz 'pilot tone, and reduces its own internal brainwave frequency to match. This is called rhythm entrainment. If the brainwave is higher than the 'pilot tone' (beat tone), say at 25 hertz, then within fifteen minutes, the brain will reduce to match the 10 hertz pilot tone which, creates a change in mood from the stress of the Beta state to the more relaxed mood of the

Alpha state. By reference, certain yogis have similar control of their brainwaves by mind control through their meditations.

The obvious advantage to using these dual tones called 'binaural tones' is the listener does not have to do anything to reach these levels by his/her own effort, other than listening. They place tones below the hearing threshold with pleasant music covering over the dual tones, helping to distract the probing aspect of the conscious mind. The benefit of this technique allows the individual to access the autonomic nervous system (the realm of the automatic levels of biological processes), to make mood changes which affects those harmful physiological moods toward beneficial behavioral changes effortlessly.

The author discovered the binaural process, mostly ignored in the mainstream of consciousness of the masses. It remains unused by anyone who might take advantage of its benefits. Unfortunately, this technology never got seriously pursued.

The author continues to do research and explore the potential of this technique and how it might apply to deprogramming unconscious scripts known in psychology to have important behavioral effects, helping eliminate phobias, and or traumas. Some studies revealed low frequencies applied electrically to the cranium (CES), can help reduce addictions. Further, the author is also experimenting with other sense imports that suggest an even greater chance for entire brain synchrony, such as light stimulation, and the use of pulsed electromagnetic fields.

Electromagnetic fields could affect the neural networks by influencing the electrical impulses across the entire brain, perhaps even influence the two endocrine glands positioned within the brain, the pineal and pituitary. These glands secrete systemically compounds that can alter the perception and may play a role in the imagination's use, a significant adjunct to dreams and lucid dreaming. Photonic stimulation at different frequencies through the eyes can have the same effect as audible frequencies, except in the visual cortex.

Photonic stimulation has also been used to

augment pituitary stimulation to offset the effects of low light level depression (chronic poor sunlight) caused by the northern parts of the globe.

What Are Dreams

Primarily dreams are mental constructions involving people, places and objects strung together to form a meaningful management of loose and unconnected data from the day or they can also be reactions to information that comes from outside of the individual's daily experience such as, premonitions, hunches and or insights and euphonies.

Dreams can originate from the fringe of the Astral kingdom, which may include visions of the future or the past. This is unusual and considered as a separate subject of discussion, or what may be called precognitive dreaming.

Most dreams are merely snippets, brief and often passing visions quixotically appearing in the half-awake consciousness of the mind. These apparitions appear then just after you fall asleep or just before you come awake in the morning. The deeper stages of sleep relative to brain wave frequencies in the delta range (1 - 4 cycles per second). Lighter ranges of sleep occur in the lower alpha and higher Theta frequencies (4 - 7 cycles per second). A phenomenon called the 'REM' state reflects the possibility of dreaming because of the registering of Rapid Eye-Movement.

We can see dreams in vivid color or black and white or maybe a combination of the two. Most people dream in color.

The best analysis of normal dreaming conditions are; is the geometry or the relative size, shape, and position of objects, people, places, etc., accurate? Usually, there's experienced a distorted relationship due primarily to the emotional attachments between the dreamer and those items seen in a dream.

For example, items or people will appear closer or larger, buildings may be in the wrong place or have distorted sizes and shapes. The fundamental experience shows only a pair of eyes floating along and witnessing only the scenery or action going on in a dream. Occasionally, sounds, such as someone talking or traffic noise and or music playing in the background. Also, certain attributes displayed with known people may be different, such as hair color, size and shape of their body, what they may wear in terms of attire.

Most often, dream content can represent a singular

concept or thought he heard or seen throughout the day, that could be a subconscious trigger, or a frustration from an incomplete altercation with someone at work or in a familial environment.

Recently, neuroscientists talk about reality. They suggest that our physical reality is not real, that it is a construct like a virtual digital reality. They say this because the mathematical algorithms that define a digital virtual reality follow the same mathematical formulas that describe physical reality.

Further, the relationship to reality solely depends on the perceiver of the reality, that depends on the accuracy of the five senses used by the observer. Now, diving deeper into this concept, we can see that verification of what we perceive becomes subject to and dependent on the eye of the beholder.

Lucid dreams make use of all five senses. So can we apply the same rules for verification when what seems real does not actually apply? Hence, dreams are not real because we can wake to another reality, a reality we all come to know and trust as real.

Logically speaking, while a subject places a virtual helmet on their head and could view the scene with no visual obstructions and they projected it at 60 frames per second in very high resolution, one could not tell the difference until removing the helmet.

Dreams originate from imagination, or the creation of images and sounds. If one daydreams of laying on a beach, listening to the waves lap upon the shore, feeling the warmth of the sun beating down on the body, and they are lucidly involved becoming completely unaware of their surroundings, they are experiencing virtual reality and to the individual; it was genuine enough.

So, controlled, lucid dreaming can provide all the benefits of reality and as many spiritual teachers advocate, dreams can be real too.

Dreams can become tools to motivate, to create, to invent new things, such as when an architect visualizes a new design for a city complex, it starts as a dream and, in time, becomes loaded with greater detail until someone builds the city.

The term 'dream' then becomes a generalized category that encompasses all things imaginary. When a child imagines themselves as an Indian warrior or an astronaut, what they see and mold from the reality they are in is just as real and entertaining to them, and it's called 'playing'. If this were not so, then children would not engage in 'play'. This behavior is very significant and critical to maturation and individual development when the child becomes as an adult. A human that cannot imagine is severely limited and perhaps defined as one dimensional.

The point here is, to allow dreaming in any form opens the doors of perception to allow for the introduction to other realities beyond the one we hang onto here.

Dreaming is as important as eating or sleeping and we should welcome this attribute into our lives as a gift, and that is so true. None of the other animals dream as we can because they are not self-aware.

What is Lucidity

Dreams come in two varieties: Those dream experiences where you are an observer mostly, wandering around like a pair of eyeballs only, with only one sensory input, sight. The second type of dream is more involved, that is, almost all five senses are in play, meaning hearing, sight, touch, even taste and smell. When this happens, the dream sequence becomes more realistic and vivid. These lucid dreams are more easily remembered as well.

Even the surroundings in the dream are detailed and more importantly, accurate in every detail, close to the same condition in the waking state. This level of sleep and the level of the dream usually becomes more epic like. Because this kind of dream is more vivid, it remains in the wideawake state as clearly as remembering an outing with a family the day before.

This kind of dream occurs very rarely. For most people, the lucid dream usually carries a strong message for the dreamer, in one form or another. Sometimes is shared by more than one person simultaneously, sensing aspects of all five senses. Prognostications (future situations, foretelling the near future) usually shape the circumstances around an event with a foreboding disaster befalling the dreamer and possibly close members of the family, or someone close to the dreamer, like a good friend serve as a warning.

These experiences also seem to be related to deeper sleep states and yield a very lucid experience. Instead of disconnected snippets, Lucid dreams tend to be epic in length and enjoy a theme or story. The surrounding environment is crystal clear, sounds are stark and crisp. The lighting and colors are quite vivid. Usually the lighting involves bright lights and a dazzling display of a full range of colors. The dreamer feels very cogent and alert while perhaps witnessing a shocking or outrageous situation, occurring right before their eyes.

Lucid dreams may present objects, animals, or peculiar situations that may represent subtle messages from the subconscious mind. The dreamer needs to pay close attention to what ispresented as there can be an underlying message or euphony for the observer.

The subconscious part of the mind is, by its nature,

is somewhat mysterious and apparently inaccessible to the reach of the conscious part of the mind. The subconscious tends to be factual and simplistic in its interpretation of external experience or input. In other words, it takes communications in a literal fashion, subtle nuances are not involved.

One of the problems with the practice of hypnosis is something called post hypnotic suggestions. Sometimes, suggestions to influence the subconscious behavior goes awry when what is suggested, carries subtle nuances of the hypnotist's concepts and the subconscious of the subject does not take away what has been given in the way intended, which can bring about aberrant reactions and or unexpected behavior.

On the other hand, if handled properly, hypnosis or self-hypnosis, which is even better, can be extremely helpful with dream practice.

The other component intricately connected to lucidity in dreams is the emotional context to the subject of the dream. In other words, the attitude about dreaming of something can be significant to the success of the target dream. This means that the dreamer must see that the control of the dream relies on the fact that the dreamer knows they can control the phenomenon.

This idea of control also lends itself to another proven idea that if for some reason a dream is interrupted, it becomes possible when returning to the bed, to pick up where one left off at the point of interruption.

Another less common experience is to re-enter a dream at some later time only to find that 'real' time within the dream has continued beyond the dreamer's awareness. It can be a shock to discover that dreams have their own reality separate from the dreamer. This idea lends credence to the independent reality of the dream universe.

Further, to add to the bizarre aspects of dream reality, someone known within a dream could die for some reason. Later that individual that died will no longer appear in that future dream sequence.

Another oddity in the dream reality is a spiritual entity can appear as an animal, like a dog or a horse solely to prevent the psychological effect of delivering a message coming from a stranger or even more profound image such as an angel or alien entity.

***

Exercises:

1. Take a 30 - 60 minute nap before attempting to engage in advanced dreaming techniques.

2. Keep a notebook, for recording dreams as well as taking notes about the day's events immediately after work, or before dinner. Keep the notebook by the nightstand, to jot down notes about any dreams immediately right after one awakes.

3. Before attempting intentional dream practice, spend 3-5 minutes of deep connected breaths. Lay on a couch or bed with head propped up slightly on a pillow.

Subtle Bodies vs. the physical Body

According to many ancient esoteric sources, the physical body is only a surface aspect of the totality of the human being. Significant components to the human are unseen, meaning these other significant components rest in their own dimensions and separated by frequency.

The autonomic nervous system, part of the parasympathetic nerve complex, sits aside from the primary or sympathetic nerve complex. The parasympathetic verve system governs many of the functions of vital organs and the endocrine system.

Depending on which resource one examines, the specific descriptions vary. In the East Indian spiritual system describes these subtle qualities defined by what are called Chakras (the Indian definition for Chakra is energy points positioned along the spine) at very specific locations and visualized as varied petaled lotus blossoms, which correspond roughly to the location of nerve complexes. There are 6 of these centers and one that sits just above the crown of the head.

In older civilizations such as Atlantis, they define the description as windows called Puukas. The

Subtle Bodies vs. the physical Body

spiritual practices involved in the first system case, relates to these points being open or closed, whereas, in the Atlantean system, energy flows from one window to another and are always open, but in the spiritual practice involves learning how to balance the energy flow across all the Puukas.

The number of subtle components are the same, meaning 6 subtle bodies within and one subtle body hovering just above the crown of the head The relative position of each center or window begins at the base of the spine, then a center or window at a point just below the navel, next a point at the stomach, next a point at the heart, then a point at the throat, next is a point at the brow roughly between the eyes, and finally a center or window just above the crown.

The first subtle body corresponds to the life force and the gate of life at the 5th lumbar. The second subtle body relates to the 5 elements; earth, fire, water, air and spirit. The third subtle body has to do with the brain in the gut, or belly brain, it rules the consciousness of inner will.

The fourth subtle body sets at the heart center

and rules the heart and emotions. The fifth subtle body sits at the throat and governs receptivity and expression. The sixth subtle body sits at the brow and corresponds to the pineal and pituitary and governs insight and clairvoyance, otherwise known as the third eye, or eye of Horus in Egyptian theology. The seventh subtle body sits just above the crown and governs wisdom and connects to the divine quantum.

The subtle body at the second level is the Astral body, The subtle body at the midpoint or third level is the mental body, The subtle body at the fourth level is the etheric subtle body and the subtle body at the fifth level is the inter-etheric subtle body, the subtle body at the sixth level is the Causal subtle body.

In this text, we are interested in the Astral body. In some of the mystical circles, they advocate that the Etheric subtle body travels, but it represents a misconception of the ancient texts and the one who advocated this idea is the leader of the Theosophical Society, Madam Helena Blavatsky.

The Etheric subtle body is stationary and governs

Subtle Bodies vs. the physical Body

all information streaming from any other dimensions as well as regulating the voice box, and the unnamed organ for communications to the elements and other beings on a telepathic level. The Atlantean term for this subtle body is called Ptkah, pronounced (pit -Kah). By its intonation, if you say it, the first syllable feels as a vacuum because the sound gets sucked into the throat, whereas the second syllable pushes the sound out and away, hence the verbal expression from the throat.

Seeing the Astral body is easy under certain circumstances. It has a slight blue color. Since the Astral sits within the physical shell (like a ghost within the shell) Its presence is best seen in a darkened room, and the Astral body is the easiest to be stimulated because of its proximity to the physical.

So, to stimulate this subtle body, some applied stress is necessary. The nature of the stress is from an act of will. For example, take a small hand towel and hold it in both hands and wring it as though you are trying to wring it completely dry. Do this for 3-5 minutes until you feel your hands are hot and feeling tingling sensations.

Now enter a darkened room (not completely dark, but no sunlight enters the space). Place your hands close together and you will see the Astral filaments reach out from each hand and connect with the filaments coming from the other hand.

The streamers are a light blue. Now hold one hand against a backdrop of no color such as the ceiling. If you focus your eyes in a relaxed way and study the edge of the fingers, especially at the tips, you will see a smoky light blue film extending beyond the skin of the fingers,

This is the outer periphery of the Astral skin. Were the Astral body to separate it would look just like the physical body but all blue and somewhat transparent. This appearance is true even for any living thing such as a plant.

There was an experiment performed many years ago at the turn of the century, by a Soviet inventor Semyon Daviovich Kirlian. His invention, by name, is Kirlian photography. By Charging photographic plates with Static electricity, we can see The Astral energy.

Subtle Bodies vs. the physical Body

More remarkably, when cutting a leaf in half, and the cutaway removed, the cutaway side still exists as the astral component. This energetic effect puzzles someone with an amputated leg, as the individual still feels the missing leg itching.

This kind of photography has remained in the fringe area of scientific research used mainly for the circus environments such as whole life expos showing alternate health practices. The Most important idea is revealing that one or more of the subtle bodies exist. Their interaction with the electrical energy produces multiple colors around the head in the photograph. Mainstream science still scoffs at the existence of subtle bodies and regards the idea as fake or not genuine science. That is unfortunate.

The Astral Body

The term Astral Field describes the subtle body relating to the Astral reality and the radiation from the Astral body itself. The body has all the properties of the Astral Kingdom, from which all Astral entities live. It has a specific low density, meaning the space is larger within the field. You cannot see the Astral Kingdom with the visual acuity of a normal human being. Even with perfect vision, we will not see the Astral. The main reason for this, as mentioned before, the molecular structure of the Astral kingdom spreads out or is more rarified and operating at a higher frequency.

The Astral body can vibrate at two different frequencies. It is the only subtle body that does this. As mentioned before, it needs to live alongside or within the physical, so it vibrates close to that frequency. When it needs to leave the physical, it adjusts its vibration to that of the Astral. Children up to the age of hormone development (adolescence) can invoke a change in frequency and follow the Astral on its way to the Astral Kingdom. This is often because the child's mind is more supple and able to embrace the impossible.

The Astral Body

The two dimensions intersect from time to time (meaning the physical and Astral) but with little consequence. The other dimensions also cross and overlap too with even less of an effect on the physical plane. Ghostly apparitions are the exception.

The Astral Body then represents a localized aspect, a component of the entire subtle human being that can move around and navigate through the Astral Kingdom. The Astral Kingdom is the ever-streaming flow of Astral Quality, a dimension resembling water like a river running its course through all the other dimensions. It needs access to all dimensions because all that the Astral body carries apply to all other parts of other dimensions too.

It is the Astral body perceiving ethereal visions of the Astral, such as souls drifting around within the Astral realm of the earth. These beings are also called disembodied spirits. The Astral body handles hunches, futuristic visions, including psychic abilities, such as Clairaudience (voices from the other side), Clairvoyance (visions from the other side, additional subtle effects of contact with other astral bodies which can give rise to other lifetimes (past lives) that may be shared with another, who may be a complete stranger in the present lifetime.

One might ask, the Astral body wears what kind of clothing? It doesn't have a special robe or unique attire for the Astral. It will typically mimic what the physical body wore on that day.

Other questions that may arise are: what does the Astral eat? Nothing! Or does the Astral body need to breathe air? No! As I mentioned, traveling in outer space did not require breathing or dawning a space suit. The Astral body could fly into and out of the sun without harm. I have noticed that after a while, the Astral body feels weary, not exactly tired as in the physical body case. So, considering endless journeys one needs to prepare beforehand.

Taoist monks that have achieved mastery of such abilities alter their eating habits, sleeping habits. Some monks leave the body for years, but this requires a change in the red blood cell count, leaving only white cells. The term within the Taoist community is an adept monk will have blood white like milk. His dwelling will have neither a kitchen, a bathroom, or a bed to sleep in. During the Northern Expedition of the Sino-Tibetan war, General Chiang Kai-shek found hundreds of monks stashed in dusty corners in isolated monasteries, covered in cob and spider webs. The general's reaction to this news from his adjutants that reported their existence, they wondered what to do with the monk's bodies. The general said, "burn them all, they'll only be trouble for us if they awaken."

So, in Asia, out-of-body travel is quite common amongst Taoist and Tibetan monks. They have specific tasks that could take years to accomplish. That practice is not an aspect advocated in this book.

I have referenced information from Wikipedia correlating several sources of esoteric philosophy, including the Theosophical Society treatises from Madam Blavatsky, Annie Basant, Alice Bailey,.etc. Also, I have referenced sources of the Christian Old Testament and the Tanakh of the Hebrew Bible.

That said, the author believes that the Old Testament is a rewritten Hebrew testament from much older documents of the Sumer records called the Enuma Alish, the creation account, inscribed 5,000 years before. I believe the Old Testament is taken from the Sumer records during the time of incarceration of the Hebrews in Babylon, from 597 bce-538 bce, after the defeat of Judah by the Babylonians.

In my first out-of-body experience, I did not see a cord of any kind. Later, during my training with the Rosicrucian Mystical Order, they only referenced the Hebrew Bible and some esoteric sources from the Temple of Karnak, in Egypt. I spent some time looking for this cord they spoke of and I found no evidence of such a cord, physical or Astral. It is my belief that this concept comes from philosophic diatribes of ancient Greece and Egypt.

There is no Astral cord but a spiritual connection (in today's terms as a 'wireless connection' to the divine Quantum. (a parallel to the idea of Wi-Fi to the cloud). That the Astral body is limited to 50 meters away from the physical body is preposterous.

I am living proof of invalidating that idea, since I traveled light years away from earth in one of my journeys, and going to New York, Chicago and Paris from Indiana, for God's sake, is just a little further than 50 meters. The truth here is, traveling out of the body is more or less safe.

Of course, in death, the connection to the physical realm breaks. In all my spiritual investigations, no one has died because of travel out of the body. Even my 15 years of training with a Taoist master, who traveled out of the body all the time, never mentioned a distance limit. Also, keep in mind, time and space do not exist in the subtle realms. So the idea is mute.

During astral projection and out-of-body experiences, some claim they can (at will or otherwise) see a silver cord linking their astral form to their physical body. This cord mainly appears to a beginning projector as an assurance they will not become lost. However, even experienced projectors find it useful, claiming it is a fast way to return to the body. This idea has no merit.

Bellallabene, unlike some astral projectors who claim to travel great distances, stated that the cord not only serves as a link between the two bodies, but it also limits the astral body from wandering great distances, describing his experience that as the astral body moves farther away from the physical body and reaches a distance of "50 to 70 meters," the silver cord pulls the astral form right back into the physical body.

Others asserted, though, that the cases of silver cord observations during out-of-body experiences and astral projections are rare; rather, no astral body observed, and the projector sees himself or herself as a "disembodied awareness or a point of view" in most cases.

We compare passing through a tunnel to the birth canal, and the silver cord resembling the umbilical cord. These are a few observations during out-of-body experiences that are sometimes likened to childbirth.

"Birth theories" hypothesized that people who got delivered by Caesarean section do not have tunnel experiences during astral projections. One study showed that there is no discrepancy between the experiences observed by people who are born through Caesarean section and those born naturally during their OBE or astral projection.

The attachment point of the cord to the astral body differs, not only between projectors but also from projection to projection. These points correspond to major chakra positions. According to the observations of Robert Bruce, there is not a single point of connection to the denser body, but a locally converging collection of strands leading out of all the major chakras, and some minor ones.

Mystics mention the silver cord, especially in contexts of dying and of near-death experiences. It is said that the cord must remain connected to the astral and the physical bodies during the projection, because if it breaks, the projector will

If a person gets older or if their death is near, the astral body slowly separates itself from the physical body and the silver cord breaks, making a complete and irreversible separation of the two bodies. In this situation, we interpret the idea of death and dying as a "permanent astral projection that cannot reverse."

Theosophical writings also interpret the words of some prophets and soothsayers in ancient times as descriptions of seeing the silver cord during their out-of-body experiences. Here again, the author is ready to dispute this idea as pure mythology.

The Astral Kingdom

The Astral Kingdom Is unlike the other subtle realms. They fix all the others' regions relating to their own qualities and vibrating at their own higher frequencies. Typically, an entity will stay within their own field and not wonder off. There are no walls that would define, physically, the boundaries. If a subtle body would move from the metal plane, they could enter the Etheric plane, but because of the difference in frequency, the mental body could not stay for very long as it would become very irritating.

The major difference is that the Astral plane or kingdom is more like a river, akin to the Greek River of Styx. The river flows through all the kingdoms. This is the river where the infamous ferryman navigates to all the kingdoms. So, also the Astral body can navigate the Astral River easily because it radiates that synchronous vibration. The purpose for the Astral body moving through all the kingdoms or planes of vibration is it has the job of returning the records kept because of the Astral body making the recordings of existence on all planes of existence.

As an Astral traveler, meaning the physical mind attaches to the Astral when it leaves the body, or, as I mentioned, it expands and contracts when 'leaving'. So, as an Astral traveler, now it becomes possible to go to all areas of the Astral River where-ever it meanders through the higher planes.

The Astral Kingdom will reveal the Astral reality of all worlds in the universe, exhibiting all the wonders of all of reality. So, you might imagine the benefits of moving around and through this realm.

Teachers exist on all levels, the Angelic realms representing all the Angelic tribes, and there are many. The Astral component of all souled beings can be found as well as their higher counterparts in the higher worlds. Be aware, however, that communicating with higher beings can be problematic because their consciousness is so much higher and spiritually advanced, the average traveler would be confused and not understand those creatures above the human level of understanding.

That said, that means you might become more

The Astral Kingdom

aware of the truth as compared to the mythologies and misinformation that is given to humans. So, you could be in for a shock and it will change your viewpoint in your normal life on the physical earth when you return from these journeys into the higher worlds.

What is Consciousness, Self-Awareness

Consciousness represents many levels of awareness. There is a little game that I find fascinating. It presents an example of active dynamic awareness. If you place the index finger of the left hand against the index finger of the right hand. Then focus on the touching of the skin between the two fingers. What is interesting about this exercise is determining where the awareness lies.

That both fingers have touch sensitivity, then either finger can feel the other. In fact, we assume that both fingers touch each other, and we assume the sensation to be identical and simultaneous.

If you focus only on the left feeling the right, the left finger will become dominant. But with a shift of focus toward the right finger feeling the left, then the right finger becomes dominant. So, the awareness depends on the mental direction of the sense feeling.

In the sense's case of sight, the awareness of objects in a space totally depends on the focus of the observer. Then, if the observer maintains a broad view of the space, it becomes possible for most, if not all, we can identify those objects.

However, when the focus distracts from the view of the room, then it becomes possible to miss several objects present. Not just to miss them, but not see them at all. When one is searching for something, it is key that the observer is not thinking of another object in mind and subsequently, will not see the object in their search, in effect blinded by the preconceived item in the observer's mind.

The effect of the mind's directive can narrow any of the five senses. If an observer is listening to a conversation, and we misinterpreted some part of what is being said. The author believes this is because the observer is not listening. The reason may be because of the observer's attention is not completely focused on the outer periphery but is also listening to what his mind is saying as he listens to the one speaking. Either the observer is calculating a response, or the inner beliefs are active and quietly disagree with the speaker's comments.

Other attributes can also interfere with awareness. If the observer is in physical pain, the pain gets pushed back or in someway reduced by not

What is Consciousness, Self-Awareness

acknowledging the pain signals from some part or all the body suffering. In the attempt to block the pain using the will, other elements of the senses will also get curtailed and reduced, thus closing one aspect of awareness will also shut down or reduce other aspects of awareness.

There are other, more generalized aspects of limiting the awareness for other areas of awareness. For example, One can acutely know themselves and what kind of clothing attire they are wearing, but as soon as they enter a room full of people also wearing the same sort of attire, the awareness shifts from a localized awareness to the group awareness and added the emotional lift and relief that the observer becomes relaxed knowing that the social environment overtakes the personal concern in favor of group acceptance.

We are all aware that people form clicks, groups formed around similar likes and dislikes and keep to small numbers. Learning how to negotiate with and navigate these social conditions is what early social skills are all about. When the observer moves between various groups without difficulty, then they are said to be socially adept.

An observer can go through life interacting with situations in the home, at work, and enjoying the company of friends while out and about attending an affair. And be completely unaware of their body and or mental state while being in the middle of a social interaction. So, another can completely know themselves and be unaware of the social interactions around them. This person may be, at the least, awkward or introverted.

In today's world, we have cell phones which corner our consciousness to focus on a small block of electronic communications held in our hands, and extend into many situations, even while driving an automobile. The irony in this, is the cell phone is a personal assistant and designed to increase the awareness of many issues we need to focus on, sadly the opposite is true. The cell phone is more of a distraction. Television is another form of intentional distraction.

We accept that plants and animals are alive and carry on their lives with a focus to survive and are aware of danger and the basic needs for survival.

Yet, unlike the human they do not possess self-awareness. Dogs are dogs and cats are cats and horses are horses, even within these three, none can imagine being another animal, such as the horse thinking of being a dog or a dog thinking of being a cat.

The human being can imagine themselves as anything other than a human. Some believe that the power to imagine is a God given gift and believed it valuable even til adulthood. It sets us humans apart from the rest of the animal kingdom. That we have the power to direct our focus and our awareness beyond the daily experience is also a superior skill found only in the human.

Dreams and Time

The element of time governs our lives. From the time we go to bed and the time we get up, we set aside time to travel to work, and we set aside time to eat lunch then we consider the trip back to the domicile, in time ready to eat dinner, then marking the broadcast time to watch our favorite television shows before returning to bed, to start the whole process all over again.

We plan outings with family, but we geared those events to allow for the coordinated effort to synchronize our time with the time that others are planning for. Planned vacations around time are not necessarily dependent on our own decisions, but based on work schedules. So, time rules our life and we are slaves to it.

Time is only relevant to the physical existence on the earth. Since Albert Einstein devised relativity, he determined that time and space are flexible as determined by certain parameters. They show the concept of the time dilation paradox where if there is increasing acceleration, then time slows down. So, for example, if an astronaut approaches the speed of light, time inside the spaceship would pass apparently normal to the passenger, but compared to earth, the time would pass more quickly, which would appear normal to people on earth.

The actual difference arises when after a year of traveling in space at the speed of light, when the ship returns to earth, and the astronaut emerges revealing that the astronaut only aged by a year, those on earth may have advanced 50 years or more. Many who consider long rang space flight realize that for the astronauts, they will have to forego ever seeing their relatives ever again, depending on the length of the voyage and the speed of the spaceship.

Other destinations that are light years away would require the astronauts to enter hibernation chambers slowing down their body processes so that when the destination arises, they will awaken to the life beyond earth. In the extreme situation, a spaceship carrying large numbers of passengers might procreate offspring along the way, then perhaps the offspring of the offspring, meaning several generations, might be necessary to reach distant worlds.

This concept, antiquated now, because technology has advanced sufficiently to glimpse a time in the future where ships can travel faster than light. The possibility of using an Einstein-Rosen bridge or wormhole could jump over vast distances in only a matter of a few moments.

In spiritual space and time, such as the Astral, there is no space or time. Here, space and time would function as one element moving at the same rate, neutralizing the effect of one against the other, which means neither one exists. The laws of physics break down as we know it. Then a whole new paradigm would exist. In theory, astronomers and astrophysicists observing the black hole phenomenon determined that this condition exists within the black hole.

When conducting out-of-body travel, the time while in the Astral could be hours when in the physical realm, perhaps only minutes have passed.

This attribute can be quite useful, depending on the need for information gotten quickly, but requires extensive time to gain that information.

So, using the Astral field as the pathway to retrieve that information is much more efficient for the needs of the physical.

In the physical world, time is linear, meaning that it moves forward only in one direction. In the Astral, everything happens at once, past, present, and future.

So, time travel is not possible yet in the physical world, but is quite possible in the Astral world. As far as dreams are concerned, the Astral body enters the Astral kingdom only after the physical consciousness is asleep. On rare occasions, the Astral body will leave while the mind may be still awake and will follow the Astral body part way into the timeless region of the Astral kingdom and momentarily glimpse the future. This is called precognition if what they have glimpsed then is remembered after awakening.

What is an OBE

An 'OBE' is an anachronism describing a separation between the Astral subtle body vacating the physical body. The sensation of the experience is quite shocking when it occurs, especially for the first time.

Here, it is the Astral body that is 'leaving'. Yet this is truly a misnomer. The subtle body doesn't leave per se, it is the passing through the physical body barrier that gives one the sensation of leaving when it is only expanding, not leaving.

Curiously, for the first time this may happen, one might think it represents the end of their life. Though the common concept is that one leaves the physical body behind at the moment of their transition, which is true, and it is the Astral body that disconnects. The caveat is, with transition, the Astral body disconnects from the physical body, but so do all the subtle bodies leave as well.

There are several subtle bodies, but we will get into that later. For the subject of this book, we will concentrate only on the Astral body behavior. Many people do not know this. The Astral body goes through the apparent separation every night for just about everyone. Of course, the conscious mind is asleep when the apparent separation occurs. There would be no memory normally of that happening in the morning after.

All manifestation is based upon vibration. The physical body vibrates at a particular frequency corresponding to the three-dimensional reality we call the world. Those aspects of the subtle realities vibrate at higher frequencies.

So, the Astral vibrates naturally to its own world called the Astral Kingdom or Astral Field. The Astral body vibrates also nearly the same as the physical body because it needs to be close at hand. It monitors daily experience and at night delivers a copy or record of that day's experience to the Akashic Record. I will also explain more about that later, too.

The difference between death or transition (here I use the term transition because death is an illusion) is the connecting link between the physical body and the Astral body. There are biblical references to the silver cord, but it is interpreted as a real element, but in truth it is a metaphor, not literal.

Since it is possible to 'travel' with the Astral body to any point in the universe, which is defined by our physicists may be greater than millions of light years across, the 'silver cord' would stretch to a limit well before that. So, there is no cord! While one may still be alive in the physical, one may go wherever one wants without limitation. This also includes other dimensions as well.

Preparing for an OBE

Perhaps this chapter is one of the most significant chapters to afford the practitioner the chance of success in leaving the physical body.

First, a certain amount of energy is required to achieve Astral projection. This means the practitioner needs to establish a baseline of rest in the physical body before attempting separation. Simply put, a nap involving perhaps an hour or two before retiring to actually sleep is very important.

Accomplishment of this action requires two states within the physical body and mind. I referred the axiom that describes this condition to body asleep with the mind awake. Body asleep means that the body needs to be completely relaxed and lying in a comfortable position with nothing that can disturb this is to be eliminated. That means no tight fitting clothing that might irritate or compress the skin to become an irritant later on. So loose fitting and lightweight clothing is recommended here.

Any external objects that might interfere with this practice also need to be removed or shut off.

These would include radios and TV. The telephone, or in this case the cell phone should be disconnected or shut off, if there is concern about losing an important call, then shut off all alerts and sound from the cell phone and keep it at least 3-4 meters (12 feet) from the body. Cell phones radiate RF energy, which can disturb the body. So, the field power falls off at the square of the distance. So, 12 feet should be sufficient.

Electrical lights and electrical wiring contribute to the household environmental disturbance. Unless you have created an electrically free space, best to turn off all electrical appliances, such as air conditioners, fans, lights, etc.

Next, plan your out-of-body experiment well in advance where the time is later in the day. Say around 7pm in the evening, when no visitors will call or visit. If you have friends or family that come around often, then it is best to inform them of your intentions to be alone, to meditate and relax. So, you are intentionally isolating any way your work might disturb what you are trying to do. Also, I don't recommend mentioning this activity to friends and family about what you are planning, lest they offer intervention out of their own disbelief or fear of you out of their concern. I still consider OBE activity strange, and scary to most people and falls way outside their paradigm of belief.

In relaxing the body, once a comfortable position gets established, then try not to move any part of your body. The idea here is to reach a point where you consciously scan any part, such as hands or feet. You should not feel them. Not numb, but bodily sensations will be absent. This means lying semi-upright with head on a pillow, but you won't feel the pillow, the bed, or any covering. Temperature can be a factor. A tepid atmosphere is pleasant, not too hot or not too cold. (The Goldy Locks temperature.)

My recommendation is to have a window open for fresh air in the room, preferably not facing on a major street with a lot of traffic running by. The air should be slightly cool.

The mind is the next hurdle. The purpose of the nap is to provide enough energy that the mind can relax without falling asleep. So, the practice should begin immediately after we conclude the nap. (perhaps the use of an alarm to awaken would be the exception.) There will be an urge to move a hand or a foot because conscious awareness that the body is present and yet not felt completely drives the curiosity further. Move some part to prove that it's still there, but you cannot feel it.

Not feeling the body is uniquely important for parts of the exercise to promote travel is to lose the sense of where you are because of the body's location senses.

The mind is a hurdle to get past because there can be many underlying thoughts about the practice, such as, is it safe to do it? The answer is absolutely. And I remind you that this process happens every night without fail. The Astral body must leave during the night to deposit the day's experience into the permanent record which lies in the Astral Kingdom.

So, it's not as though the Astral body has never done this before. It is unusual for the conscious mind to encourage the Astral to leave when the conscious mind is still awake. The Astral kingdom would not be a first destination. Usually, the Astral body will move about the earth Astral field often.

This is also a bit more exciting for the conscious mind too. First, because it will move about on the Astral earth with many limitations of physical conditions removed. Physical aches and pains will be gone. The ability to pass thru 'solid' objects is an interesting experience as well. Then the power to be unlimited by gravity is a real rush.

One of my favorite tricks is using a mirror. Setting a full mirror in front of you while you stare at your reflection sets the possibility of conscious transfer to a known target. Here, the mirror reflection can be that target. First, it's a familiar target and second, it's not far away.

So, the practice is to stare at your reflection for one to two minutes, then close the eyes and try to recall your reflected image in your mind. Imagine now that you are in the mirror looking back at the physical body. Once you have that sense, that your perception is from the mirror reflection, it becomes the stepping off point and like my original bedroom window; it becomes a doorway.

This technique can make it easier to shift out of the body in the early practice. Just picking a destination in the room or in another room can replace this technique later, the caveat there is, you will need to visualize the target as vividly as though you are there and not the bed.

The first alchemical rule — you are where you think. For finding a friend or looking for someone, then you need that same focus and vividness.

I found I could imagine a hole in the ceiling for which I could project myself through.

Also, another target zone that is good for beginning practice is underwater. Since breathing is not an issue, being under warm tropical water is very soothing and promotes a good foundation.

Now let's talk about exit points. Believe it or not, there are several. The classic exit point is between the eyebrows. Another is out of the top of the head. I found the most common place to exit from is the solar plexus just below the diaphragm. Ideally, you would like the exit to be straightforward. That is not always the case. I have fallen out the back opposite to the solar plexus. Since the separation is sudden and unexpected, the sensation is like someone allowing you to free fall through a trapdoor. In that case, try to remember to keep the eyes open, otherwise all will be blackness.

Checking that your eyes are open is important. It can be an unconscious behavior not to see the wonder before youor the horror you expect.

There can also be exits out of the feet that usually extend beyond where you are not vertical. Then you move about like you are on a gurney, sliding around.

Now let's talk about returning. It is so easy. All you need to do is think of your body back in bed. You will return with a snap. If you enter the body slowly, you may encounter thought forms hanging around your body. It depends on whether you may have some concerns in your life and you are unconsciously thinking about them. This creates Astral matter. If repeated, will generate forms that represent the powerful feelings and thoughts. If you have been apart for very long, such as hours, physical body response may be a little delayed and you won't be able to move right away as expected. Just lay there quietly with your eyes open and physical responses from the body will soon return.

It is fun to experiment with understanding friends who may be excited about being involved with your experiments. You can give them a heads up of your plan to visit them and you can practice applying telepathy or attempt some telekinetic activity to prove your presence nearby.
Then later you can compare notes.

Time Travel, Remote Viewing

Many times, leaving the body can be both deliberate and also spontaneous activated by a subtle current deep within the being. In the latter case, you may exit the body but propelled to another place you are not familiar with, even another dimension.

In that case, you will endure the experience, like it or not. I have been to some of those places which are not pleasant. In addition, it may attract the Astral body to an event in the past that was impactful and desirous to have closure. Very often, this is a past life experience.

Once, while living in New York city, I went to bed one evening and suddenly stood on a street corner near my apartment. I met a girl there who also had just arrived. I said to her, "do you know why you are here tonight?" She shook her head in the negative. Then, moments later, three young men leaped out of thin air and onto the street near where the girl and I were standing.

One of the young men turned to both of us and declared, "Are you ready?" I said, "Ready for what?" The young man smiled and declared they

Time Travel, Remote Viewing

were there to teach us how to leap into time.

This apparently depended on intentionality and an aggressive leap into the air, much in the same way the three young men had done when they arrived.

So, the three young men turned and leaped into the air and disappeared. The young girl and I also leaped but did not change location or time frame and simply landed on the street a few feet from where we leapt.

I was confused and did not understand what was going on and what they were trying to teach us. A short time passed and two of the young men returned. Then they apologized. "Okay, we are going to try this again, so pay attention. It's not that hard!" They turned away again and as I watched them carefully, I had a peculiar feeling come over me and I had the urge then to leap into the air, only this time I landed several hundred feet further away, next to the main thoroughfare which was Broadway.

It was several hours later, just a little before dawn. It was 11pm went I made the jump.

I immediately realized that I had leaped back into the past. It was 1905. There were no cars around, no busses, only horse-drawn carriages parked along the avenue. Then, I saw a carriage go by slowly. The driver was standing in the carriage dowsing the gas lanterns along the street. Across the street, I saw an old-fashioned milk wagon, horse-drawn, and the man hopped out to deliver bottles of milk to apartments along the street. I never saw the girl again and wondered momentarily, if she had been successful, too.

I walked down the avenue to the first cross street, 72nd. I crossed and proceeded along 72nd Street and came across a small store. A prominent sign displayed called WILBY'S Mercantile. I climbed the steps to the front entrance and found the door unlocked. I entered cautiously. I called out, but no one responded. The floor was wooden and creaked a bit when I entered. I passed by a rather large bright red coffee grinder with big fly wheels with spiral spokes. As I continued inside, I passed a large wooden barrel full of pickles sitting in their own juice. They smelled amazing, with an aroma of garlic.

There was a dim light coming from the rear of the store, so I made my way toward the light. As I got closer, I called out again. This time, a man's voice responded. "Sorry, I'm very busy right now. Can you come back a little later?" I said, "I couldn't help admiring your wonderful store, but my time here is limited. Do you mind if I stay for a moment and chat with you while you are working?" The proprietor chuckled and said, "I'm in my basement. Come on back but mind the stairs, there is a couple of loose boards, so watch your step."

When I descended three steps down, I chose not to go any further. I could see the man wore mutton chops as sideburns. He was slightly balding and overweight and sported a rather large handlebar mustache.

white powder covered him from head to toe. I asked what he was doing? He declared he had an idea for a new building material. But during his efforts to make it solid after baking, it would not hold up and kept crumbling. He was frustrated. I soon realized that he was attempting to create what we know in the future as sheet rock. When he told me of his ingredients, I knew what was missing. I knew he needed to add gypsum to the mix. But I anguished to tell him because I thought I might alter the future in some terrible way. So I finally said, "I believe you have a great idea there and believe that you will find the solution someday soon, and it will be a great success."

He was very thankful. I bid him farewell. Then, with my intention to return to my time, I dashed into the street, almost being run over by a model T motor car. I slipped back into my time unscathed. Then I returned to my body and slept for the rest of the night.

To this day, though I live in Arizona, I sometimes frequent the lower part of New York city in the region called SoHo, which means South of Houston Street. I always seek a small coffee shop on the corner where I get a coffee and a Danish. I walk around for a while before I return to my bed in Arizona. I do not know why I am so attracted to this spot.

I am not a great remote viewer. During some of

my meditations, I will see landscapes clearly but no clear identifying qualities. Once I rode on a train in Russia, somewhere near Vlodivostock. It didn't feel like me though, more like I was looking through someone else' eyes. These are often brief visions. Often, I will see trees and a road, but again no information about where the location is. So, this development is a work in progress.

Two Levels of the Astral Field

There are two levels of the Astral field that describe the Astral body. They are relative to the frequency of each state. As I stated before, the Astral body vibrates very close to the physical body when present. When the Astral body exits the physical, it may be operating at the physical body frequency. If that is the case, then you will know right away because the Astral cannot pass through doors or ceilings. In that case, you will need to open doors and go outside to get free of the dwelling.

The second frequency is much higher. In that case, the Astral body is completely free of any physical obstacles. The Astral may not raise its vibration right away, but as soon as it enters the Astral Kingdom, then it must equalize to the Astral Kingdom vibration.

So, if one exits the physical body and discovers that the Astral is still at the physical frequency, then one needs to return to the physical and exit again. This will usually correct this issue. And, as I mentioned, the Astral may be sluggish to return to the physical vibration upon entering as well.

Two Levels of the Astral Field

After my family's friend introduced me to the San Jose chapter of AMORC, or the American Order of the Rosy Cross, the Rosicrucian brotherhood. I learned that there were degrees of training, with tests conducted at each level to determine understanding and showing certain skills. There are 12 degrees in the Rosicrucian Order. When one reaches the 9th degree, they expected one to show their skill at Astral travel. The test was to show up at the Rosicrucian Park, where a ceremonial place is prepared for initiates to be ordained at the ceremonial site with all advanced members present, but out of body.

Once I learned to get out, I traveled from Indiana to San Jose and hung around watching people go thru the process. It wasn't long before they discovered me and told to leave. They asked if I was a student. I replied yes. Then they said, well you have showed the 9th level skill, but you haven't completed your other training. So, return when you have completed the work, then it will be your turn. It wasn't long before I realized I did not favor the philosophy of mysticism and their training. I stopped the training and never went back, feeling it just wasn't my way.

Techniques to Encourage Lucidity

Lucidity in dreams largely depends on memory. You need to awaken the awareness in your dreams. Mostly, people are only observers in their dreams and not active participants in any conscious way. They are like a pair of floating eyeballs, with ears connected sometimes.

To become lucid, you will need to engage in at least 3 of your sense faculties. But before you try that, you need to remember that you want to be more conscious.

First, to trigger that intention, you need to program yourself before you go to sleep.
That requires something odd that you will look for in your dream, something that stands out and reminds you of your original intention.

It can be anything unusual. For example, begin the day with your intention that when the night comes, you will be ready to remember your intention. So, pick a brightly colored ribbon tied around your arm or wrist. Through the day, look at the ribbon, noting the color and your intention. When you dream, you may notice that the ribbon hangs on your wrist. Then, noting to yourself about

Techniques to Encourage Lucidity

the meaning of the ribbon, look for a location in your dream where there could be a mirror, like a bathroom facility.

When you find the mirror, look carefully at yourself. Then speak to yourself and explain that you want to be fully present. As you explain, listen to your voice as you speak. Then follow by bringing your hands into view, rub them together and proclaim you can feel them, even wash them with water and dry them. Then look down at your feet, walk around and feel your footsteps.

By this time, you have engaged in at least 3 of your five senses; sight, listening, touching and speaking together with movement. From there, your dream will become clear and you will probably change the nature of the dream completely.

Another waking up trick is creating a strange animal. For example, a rabbit that is green with yellow stripes. Or look for a horse that can talk. These strange objects can be a trigger for you to remember to contact yourself.

Point to Point vs Real Time Travel

I have discovered that there are two different ways to travel in the Astral. First is point to point.

In this way, there is no awareness of passing scenery or time passing. You need to create a target. Focus on it until you can feel yourself there.

For example, going to the Grand Central Station on Lexington Avenue in New York. You would need to pick a certain spot in that location. Seeing it in the mind until it becomes a daydream.

As you continue to focus on the target, other elements can come into play, such as hearing the traffic, with horns tooting, the hustle and bustle of people rushing by, or the loudspeaker announcements of trains appearing on certain tracks. The more you bring to the dream, the more real it becomes until the Astral leaves and suddenly you are there and not aware of your original place at all. The time to travel is nothing, even if the distance is greater.

With traveling in real time, you leave your existing location consciously and travel by flight to the target. If you are traveling from New York to

California, your time of traveling may depend on how fast you want to move, so, like a bird might take quite a while to arrive. The time will pass as real time as well. I mean to make the choice to go point to point for long distances, where shorter distances can be more leisurely and you can take in the scenery on the way.

The Problem with Adolescence

As I mentioned earlier, I began my out-of-body experiences at seven. In the beginning of my conscious traveling, I cared not about how I did it since it seemed spontaneous. My conscious traveling came after my shrinking experiments. That I began when I realized I could reduce my consciousness to a point source. Then it was easy to crawl out through the tear ducts of my eyes.

As I grew older, my flying became increasingly more difficult. By the time I was eleven years old, my struggle and the need to get above a certain level from the ground revealed itself. For a while, I achieved this by finding a hill or some elevated spot, leaping off the high ground, then gave me access to the magical level where I could fly off.

I didn't realize what was happening with this apparent limitation. Over many years later, I analyzed my experience. Subconsciously, I was fighting hormones, the kind that pour into the body during the transition to adolescence. The need to climb higher from the ground showed my fight with the new hormones. The hormones were shifting me out of my childhood and into adulthood, hence grounding me in the so called 'real' world. Reaching up was my unconscious attempt to call on my pineal-pituitary to assist my freedom to fly.

Very much like the movie cartoon, I was one of the lost boys that Peter Pan took care of. I felt puzzled because Peter was the only one who could fly. They grounded the rest of the lost boys in the story. So, if a pixie brought the other boys to Neverland, why then only peter got this ability by the pixie Tinkerbell? Then later, I realized Tinkerbell was in love with Peter and was very jealous of Wendy, the older sister of her two younger brothers John and Michael.

Yes. This is just a childhood cartoon and should not matter beyond my childhood fantasies. I believe the story of Peter Pan is an archetypal representation of the inner spirit that knows it can fly. Somehow, I latched onto that character and idolized it for the better part of my early childhood. Later, it was Superman.

That is also a clue to this mystery. Superman came in as a child but grew up still being able to fly in the 'physical world'. He was Kalel, an alien from Krypton, a planet that was bigger and having greater gravity. So, when he arrived on earth, his strength and ability to fly was not really flying but jumping. As the intro line said, "able to leap tall buildings in a single bound."

So, I believe that is why I shifted heroes as I got older. The theme of flight still burned in my imagination. I held on to it in my lucid dreams, continuing to get up into the 'magical level. My attempts to overcome the limits even extended to tying a rope around a tree, running around the tree as fast as I could, unwinding the rope to fling my body into the air. Otherwise I could not reach by jumping up any longer. This extended to jumping off the roof of my house in the waking world. I tried doing this several times while wide awake. It saddened me as it forced me to be tied to the ground!

Afterward, I had given up. Once in a great while, I would lucidly dream of traveling in a car and admiring the steep rolling hills passing by. I commented to myself, these hills would be perfect to fly over. Sometimes I had success, but mostly, just disappointment.

The Illusion of Death

There is a commonly known phrase in human communications; the only thing you can count on is death and taxes!

Well, the tax part is true, but we compose the other part with religious training and eons of esoteric and group mythology. Later, as I studied esoteric mythology and yogic accounts, it seemed there might be some truth amongst all the false beliefs.

The transition process meant that ties to the physical are severed, which includes the Astral body. Once Astral travel occurs, the sense that the conscious exists beyond the body can become a rich resource of confidence regarding fears of what is called death. Einstein once declared that energy can neither be created or destroyed, but it can be transformed.

The life-force flows through the physical body like a river. There is a gate where it enters. It is called the gate of life. The point of entry is between L5 and L6 in the lower lumbar of the spine.

It pools at the base of the spine, coiled up like a

serpent. It is the source of the Kundalini, which represents the focus of Indian spiritual practice.

We could compare the physical body to a marionette or puppet. The life-force streams from the Quantum and carries the divine consciousness and directives about evolutionary development as part of the life package. It will contain all previous living experiences from all previous lifetimes. The Astral body has managed all that background for the soul to develop and work on depending on the success and failures from previous experience. The sum is the Akashic record, or book of life.

Strings connected hold the 'puppet' to the puppeteer. The strings animate the body. Of course, the metaphor of a puppeteer is only for explanation. There is no puppeteer per se. The driving force is inherent within the life-force stream as a program or set of instructions. The instruction set is dynamic. It adjusts from first day on, depending on the progress of the spiritual understanding unfolding.

It is quite possible that when an individual makes leaps in their development that exceed the intentions of the life pattern that began the life experience, on rare occasions, an individual may the receive new sets of instructions and will shift the life pattern embedded into the DNA and move on to another life experience while still existing with the same body without transitioning into another body.

This means that dormant DNA having nothing to do with the existing life will awaken or activate while the original DNA is deactivated. In effect, this establishes a new body which will take 7 years to complete.

There are specific periods when this can happen. We refer them in astrology as Saturn return cycles. Typically, this is in the human chronological ages of 28 and 56. The 56th year period is called a second Saturn return. The individual will do a mini life review, such as reconsidering a task in life like a job or relationships that can rekindle or fall away.

It does not mean necessarily that the individual alters the body beginning a whole new incarnation, but it reflects the inherent property of the DNA cycle to allow that to happen. The adding of another incarnational influence is rare. These two periods define the time when that could become possible.

There is additional support for this astronomically as well. At the time of the first Saturn cycle and at the second Saturn cycle, The stars in certain constellation alignments can be a new source of inspiration to the DNA, meaning the star fields represent different levels of consciousness with those new constellations feeding the DNA during those periods. When the influence is offered, but the individual may choose not to respond to the stimulus.

The coming together of male and female is also part of this influence all during the DNA cycling of both. This means that compatibility may be strong until a Saturn return occurs where one or both in a relationship may dissolve and they will no longer be attracted to each other.

States of Extraordinary Consciousness

There are three states of extraordinary conscious. The first is Mental Traveling or what some now call Remote Viewing. Though this aspect of consciousness can also incorporate the idea of clairvoyance. This is the ability to witness events at a distance and perhaps at another time, which would also include precognition.

Specifically, the government program describes Remote Viewing as the practice of seeking impressions about a distant or unseen subject, purportedly sensing with the mind. Typically, a remote viewer expects to give information about an object, event, person, or location that is hidden from a physical view and separated at some distance set up by coordinates as a target site.

The CIA investigated this ability to determine its viability for possible new ways to conduct espionage against hostile governments. They did not come to this on their own. The reports of the Russians already using people with these psychic abilities to spy on American activities alarmed the intelligence arm of the government and they were determined to catch up.

So, in the early 70s, the CIA began secretly exploring people who might possess these abilities. The original proponents of this activity were Russell Targ and Harold Puthoff. Later Ingo Swann, Joseph McMoneagle and Courtney Brown led the secret group and conducted many sessions peering in on Russian activities during the cold war.

The second extraordinary consciousness is Astral Traveling. This activity differs from remote viewing because the consciousness actually moves out of the body and proceeds to a distant point to observe events, places and or people.

In addition, a second aspect of Astral traveling must include Bi-location. This means that the Astral body vibration could reduce to a physical vibration while apart from the physical body. This affords others to see the Astral body and even communicate with it. Biblical accounts describe that Jeshua (Jesus) had this ability. And beyond a single manifestation, more than one projection done at the same time where groups saw Jeshua in different places simultaneously.

The third extraordinary consciousness is called teleportation. Here, the consciousness moves to a distant location and brings the physical body along by dematerializing the body and then materializing the body in the new location.

This activity is quite rare and considered, among most, as an urban legend. There have been historical accounts that are uncorroborated where this has happened. In modern times, there is no accounts that describe this phenomenon. We infer this ability is mentioned within the Yogic Aphorisms of Patanjali which details many yogic psychic powers.

The Kundalini Spiritual Practice

There is a book written by a famous Yogi adept called the 'The Aphorisms of Patanjali.'

In the book, Patanjali describes the high yoga practice called Raja Yoga. These are the spiritual exercises related to developing many psychic powers. Another Famous Yogi is Parahamsa Yogananda, as described in the book called 'Autobiography of a Yogi'. It describes his own path and some of the miraculous people he met in India showing amazing feats.

If you want to follow the Yogic way of life, then The Yoga Aphorisms of Patanjali is a major work on the practice of high yoga and meditation.

Patanjali does not discuss the more popular form of yoga called Hatha yoga, which entails all the postures and stretches that prepare for Raja Yoga.

Through these ancient aphorisms, you will learn how to control your mind and achieve inner peace and freedom. Although these methods got taught over 2,000 years ago, they are as alive and effective today as they have ever been. Then there is a unique form of yoga that is part of the Raja form that would be extreme. The breathing techniques are very hazardous without a teacher experienced in the practice.

This form is called Kundalini Yoga. It defines a spiritual practice that will encourage the energy that sits dormant at the base of the spine, likened to a serpent coiled ready to strike. When stimulated will rise upward along the spine toward its goal, the crown or top of the head. It is said that when the serpent rises, it will energize and 'awaken' all seven energy centers, bestowing the practitioner with all the esoteric magical powers. It sounds fantastic! Yet it is not so easy. The meditations are difficult to achieve and a little dangerous.

The Taoist practice also includes this aspect of yoga, it is a variation of Tibetan yoga. There are a few caveats in this form. The Taoist monks believe the sexual force contained within the serpent is toxic to the normal nervous system. So, they provide a special meditation which involves creating an imaginary iron pot or kettle, they call the caldron that sits within the naval area inside the body.

One extracts the sexual energy and pulls it in the

kettle to be cooked with special breathing techniques. If successful, it converts the raw sexual force to steam. Then the steam gets distributed through all the vital organs and nervous system until the aspirant is ready to accept the raw form direct from the serpent when it rises.

Another variation of this practice is called Bastrika yoga, (This Physical Raja) where the yogi lifts the body up while in the lotus posture on the hands. Then lowers the bottom of the spine against the floor, over and over, striking it hard many times, which is supposed to create the attention to that area by pain without the tiresome adjunct of meditation. I mention this as a reference only. I don't recommend doing it.

Years ago, I went to a yoga rounding weekend with my first wife who devoted her attention to and was enamored by the Maharishi Mahesh Yogi. He established the mindless meditation. The weekend was quite rigorous. Yoga practice 3 times a day, followed by the mindless meditation.

I knew nothing about the kundalini energy. So, to my surprise, the serpent rose along my spine

The Kundalini Spiritual Practice

uninvited, then halted at the first cervical in my neck. The energy did not stop there, however. It shot down my left arm, wrapping around my arm as a snake might. It left a double row of blisters around my arm down to the wrist, defining its track. If that wasn't bad enough, my arm was solid, like it had been quick frozen and when my previous wife tried to massage the stiff muscles, it hurt like hell, and sounded like breaking glass. So, I'm a big believer in the danger of raw sexual force running rampant around my body.

Many years later, when I studied with a Taoist master, I asked him about that experience. He said, "now imagine had that energy reached your brain, it would have been like frying eggs for your brain. So, when you are meditating, be sure to hold the tip of the tongue to the roof of the mouth. That gives the energy a safe return to the bottom of the spine without harm to you." It works for me and I recommend that to anyone interested enough to try that practice.

In the yogic practice of breathing, called Pranayama, this technique promises to stimulate the serpent as well. This practice can be very harmful if not fatal, if someone does not do it correctly. When this practice gets applied incorrectly, if it doesn't kill you, it can really make you very ill. It's shocking that they wrote down this practice for any fool to read and follow, believing it's a straight pathway to God. Perhaps this might be true, but not the way you would think. I believe this is irresponsible and dangerous. We should only try this knowledge and practice with an experienced teacher.

Adventures with Astral Travel

I lived in a small quasi-rural town in Indiana. It wasn't a 'one horse' town, but close to it. It boasted two movie theaters for a sleepy population of 20,000 people. By the age of 8 years, I kind of knew what I liked and knew my place in the household pecking order. Oddly, I felt unusually confident, avoiding undesirable situations when possible. I remained quiet in the background, feeling the need for privacy and very introspective, trying hard to stay out of trouble. But God, I could not wait to grow up and get the hell out of 'Dodge'!!

At an earlier age of 7, I didn't leave my body at first. I began exploring, changing my size and successfully reduced my size to that of an ant. I exited my tear duct and emerged onto my cheek to stare at the enormous lens and eyeball jutting out from under my brow, appearing as a great cliff where the hair fell over the edge.

My first adventure out of the body (OBE) was an accident! At 8 years of age, I felt things in my life were getting more serious. My brother was older than I by 5 years and enjoyed more privileges. One of those privileges included watching TV beyond

7:30 pm, the hour of my bedtime. It was also the time of my favorite comedy show, 'I Love Lucy'. This recurring disappointment frustrated me, also exacerbated by my brother's taunting humiliation. I stormed to my bedroom upstairs, sulking until I fell asleep.

I entered the dream world, but still aware of my bedroom around me. With my desperation and anger, I still wanted to run away. I jumped from my bed and opened the window to climb out. Looking down sent a shiver up my spine. It was a fifteen-foot drop to the ground. Then I gulped, ready to jump down to the ground to make a clean getaway. Nervously, I let go of the windowsill and pushed off. I expected the awful thrill of falling. Instead, I just hung motionless in midair, floating high above the ground, illuminated by the soft moonlight.

Stunned at first, I felt awe and excitement that I could float in mid-air. This was significant to any kid at that age. Peter Pan enamored me, flying like a bird and Superman leaping over tall buildings in a single bound.

I looked back over my shoulder into the window to see my body still lying in the bed. I wondered what caused this. My interest in leaving still outweighed my curiosity to understand what I saw. I was so thankful anyway for the 'help' to escape my situation. Holding my terror and breath, I flew away from my house like Peter would have done, with great joy and glee that I had somehow outsmarted my enemies (my brother and my parents).While flying, I pondered if Never Neverland existed.

Flying in the air and feeling everything so lucidly was an amazing feeling! My idol, Pan, made swimming motions with his arms to fly. So, I too moved my arms in the same way. My body sailed through the air effortlessly, feeling the cool night air moving past my face, ruffling through my pajamas as I moved higher and faster.

Then I realized a ridiculous conundrum: I love to fly like a bird, yet I have a fear of heights! Realizing this, my fear of heights countered and limited my joy and pleasure while using this new ability. I wanted to break away from my fear of heights boldly, but caution and prudence won the day. It kept me close to the ground, safe and just above the trees.

I traveled beyond our farm (a two-story three-bedroom cedar shake covered house on 100 acres.) The land sported a huge apple orchard, some livestock including 5 cows, 75 pigs, a dog, two geese, a horse, some chickens, and a large cornfield).

I mowed the lawn, fed the animals, hoed the garden from time to time, but hated my chores and farm life. I could not easily get to my friends on foot, so a steady lonely feeling intensified the need to get away. I flew silently in the night, past the neighborhood to Meridian Street, the main rode into town.

I could see people walking on the sidewalk below me. I could hear them talking, but when I called out, they didn't respond. I was a silent birdman flying above them. I continued flying around town, taking in the view from above. I was having so much fun. I grew tired after a while and my anger and frustration passed, so after several hours, I returned home, back through the open window. I don't remember slipping back into my body and awakened in the morning trying desperately to hold on to my secret and thinking about the adventure continuing in the next evening.

It came time for my going to bed, only this time I rushed up the stairs and got right into bed and anxiously closed my eyes. I think my parents, at least my mother and brother, were a little stunned by my new behavior. I left the window open to make my escape more silent. Then, after some time passed, I was already at the window ledge, ready to jump into my next nighttime adventure.

My fear was now nonexistent. I flew higher and higher and realized I had left the atmosphere of the earth. I hung in space looking at the earth. The scale, of course, was not so accurate, but I estimated I was approximately apart by about 4,000 miles, as the earth in size was equal to holding a basketball in your hands up close.

I looked over my left shoulder to see the moon brightly lit, but the moon was not quite full yet. I enjoyed the light from it and it felt warm and fuzzy. There was an urge to leave and go deeply into space without the slightest idea where I would go exactly. I hesitated, and a fresh fear came over me. I wondered about getting lost amongst the stars and never finding earth again. Then decided I wasn't ready for the journey yet. This situation occurred two more times when I wouldn't leave.

Then on the fourth night, I felt a certain sense of cavalier bravery and boldly let go of my fear and took off like a rocket. I didn't bother moving my arms as before, and realized I could use my mind to travel faster by only thinking of it.

The journey was magnificent, passing by big red suns and so many blue dwarf stars dangling among the gas clouds of many colors. On this journey, I traveled in real time. Later, I discovered there are other, more efficient ways to get around. Finally, after approximately 4 hours, I landed on a planet.

The landscape appeared as rolling hills but very rocky, with a few strange trees popping up from time to time. They were smooth without bark and the leaves looked like kale, all shriveled with small, cupped petals, looking like purple cabbage.

And the trunks of these trees were multicolored in purple hues resembling an oil slick. The grounds illuminated by a soft light, but I could not see any observable sources of light.

I came upon a small clearing that rose higher than the ground nearby and there, sat upon the upper surface, a large thick stone table with a few stone stools sitting around. I felt a little tired and took one stool to sit on. A few moments later, a person of rather large stature appeared and set the table for one, that was something to eat for me.

This person dressed in a hooded robe, perhaps black, but the light was too dim to tell. The man spoke to me, telling me I should eat quickly because I needed to return to earth. I complained. I spent hours getting there and now I must leave so soon?

The person said, "It's remarkable, you came here now, but you are way too early, and you can not stay." My arrival convinced this person I would return someday. Then I could stay longer. I had so many questions to ask, but he refused to answer and bid me a fond farewell and a good journey back. I arrived back home, but it was almost daylight. I was exhausted and fortunate to return to my bed, while everyone was still sleeping.

I slipped back into bed and then opened my eyes, feeling so exhausted from the journey. I never went back. I will never forget the experience as it remains as lucid to me now as when I traveled, and that was 70 years ago.

After this adventure, my boldness blossomed. I began at 9 to travel to Chicago, New York, even crossed the Atlantic to visit Paris. Traveling over water seemed to be troublesome. I had to work very hard to stay aloft. When I arrived in Paris, I was circling near the top of the Eiffel tower. My fear of heights rejoined me, so I descended to a bridge that crossed the Seine river. I landed in front of the third lamp post. The lamp post was very ornate and covered with several globe shaped balls of white light. I turned to look over my left shoulder and there, perched above the distant trees, was the Eiffel tower.

Many years later, I returned to France in the physical. I spent the better part of a day looking for that bridge. It turns out there are many bridges that cross the seine river. Finally, a French taxi told me that the bridge I was describing was the Alexander the III bridge. So, I had to know. I approached the third lamp from the end. My body shook uncontrollably. Then, standing on the exact spot where I landed, I turned to look over my left shoulder to see the Eiffel tower standing exactly where I had seen it in the Astral. Proof that my travel was real!

When I was 13, there was a friend of the family, a deacon of the church that we attended, came by the farmhouse to have a cup of coffee and chat a while with my parents.

Making home movies was a favorite hobby, trying to duplicate some of my favorite horror movies. I built a couple of Egyptian statues in my bedroom as props for a mummy movie. I invited the family friend to come and see what I created.

He was shocked and said that he and I needed to talk about things he was doing, but he did not want to reveal what that was with the rest of the family. Later, he told me he had been a member of the secret Rosicrucian Order, out of San Jose, California. When he saw that I possessed a keen interest in Egyptian culture, he felt I should join and learn about mysticism.

Two years later, while visiting my brother and attending high school in California, I used some techniques for traveling to go to Indiana and join in discussion with this man on a park bench a few nights a week. My brother was a staunch nonbeliever with all this, until I received a letter from the man in Indiana, exclaiming how much he enjoyed our nightly meetings in Indiana.

My brother worked for North American Aviation at the missile plant. His job was to calibrate the gyroscopes for the missiles. To prove my point, I traveled to the plant, then entered the top-secret facility. I went to his workbench and copied the serial number from the gyro he was working on.

I returned to Indiana. Later, while attempting to use a technique for reaching someone directly with Astral travel, I thought of my sister, who lived in San Diego, California. Suddenly, I ended up sitting on her living room floor for a few brief moments, long enough for her to glimpse me before I disappeared. She was shocked to see me and called out my name.

This was my one and only experience of bilocation. It delighted me. I was successful. I have found this technique quite challenging. Given the stories of Jeshua bi-locating, not once but several times and simultaneously appearing in different places, I can certainly appreciate his skill level. Probably the reason the Romans had such a difficult time trying to capture him.

A few years ago, I was driving on the Taconic highway in New York, returning from a conference in Massachusetts. When I rounded a turn, suddenly I was apart, hanging out near my driver side rear view mirror watching me drive from outside. This situation was like changing your view in a racing video game. I did not enjoy that experience.

I freaked out for the moment trying to command my Astral to re-enter, as it were, for fear I would lose control of the car. It was an unfounded fear because that part of my mind had not changed its focus on driving the car.

I mention this because we are programmed to accept the viewpoint only from within the physical body. If, and when, you want to practice this spiritual skill, sometimes the Astral takes upon itself to separate ad hoc. So be aware this can happen.

Contacting Another Person

One of my favorite aspects about traveling out of the body is using that skill to reach out to someone known to you. Should you desire for them to contact you when you cannot reach them by ordinary means? This technique can be a lifesaving skill in an emergency.

The first step is to visualize that person in your mind while you are apart in the Astral realm. This will have the effect of drawing you to them where-ever they may be. So, you do not need to know where they live. If they would be out and about, then you will draw to their exact location, even when you are unaware of the location.

After you arrive at the location where the friend or relative is in the moment, you can enter their mind because you are at very close range and you can give them the thought to reach out to you, giving them your contact information.

As an example, someone becomes stranded by the road after their transportation breaks down. It is possible for you to travel to their location, send them your thoughts and your personal identification.

They may be worried, so it can be an effort to break through to their subconscious. But you must keep applying your thought to them. They may be resistant at first, but your constant effort will pay off. Then, if they need medical attention, you can travel to the nearest medical facility or police department.

Then you will need to contact a stranger in the same way as before, conveying simple key statements revealing the location of the friend or family member in desperate need. Unlike contact with someone you know, you will need to approach several people perhaps, enter their body and mind to get a sense if they are open-minded. Once you find that person, then go into their mind and relay the critical information. I realize this idea would seem preposterous if not impossible, but it is possible. Perhaps in an emergency, bilocation might be better.

We can also use this technique on oneself. It becomes possible to reach the subconscious of oneself while outside of the body. Then apply the same mental suggestions to provide influential statements that could override unconscious behavior patterns that cause difficulty in the waking life.

One other positive aspect of this technique is reaching out in the Astral field to contact your spiritual guide. There are spiritual guides that roam the Astral Kingdom. They are on the lookout for individuals who, by their efforts, will attract the teacher they need. Using your will desire to call upon them can be quite rewarding. Many guides are also on the lookout for those who are not ready, and they place them back into their bodies. This might be where the 50 meter distance comes into play.

There are groups of people who can do this. Often, they will meet out of body at some designated place they all agree to. Then they will discuss aspects of spiritual understanding that can only be expressed out of the body. Some are explorers and will travel together to difficult places that may reveal unique historical sites and or information.

Last, if one feels courageous and so desires to

travel out of body to other planets and meeting with extraterrestrials is also possible. Overcoming the resistance to leave earth is the only stumbling block to this activity. So, like myself, you may need to make several attempts before success. Once contact occurs, they are very interested in people who can do this. There are those entities that would welcome an exchange and may come to you as well.

This kind of activity is extremely beneficial as it will open the mind and the heart to the reality that the universe is teaming with intelligent life. It gives the greater sense of a larger family and a strong feeling of belonging to something beyond earth.

Bilocation

Bilocation is a term, as it implies, to be in two places at the same time. It represents the third of four phases of the spiritual process of 'teleportation' (the ability to dematerialize the physical body and transport it to another location where the body then re-materializes). This concept has remained in the realm of the impossible fantasy.

The first aspect is moving the mind (remote viewing as in psychic spying) or mental traveling. Then second phase, leaving the physical body behind with the Astral subtle body and traveling to other locations.

The third phase is making the Astral subtle body visible to others while at the projected destination. They have recorded this aspect of spiritual power in the New Testament, where Jeshua (also known as Jesus) appeared in several places to give sermons to the people. He accomplished this by first Astral traveling out of his physical body, then downloading his Astral body's vibration to the three-dimensional vibration in order to be seen and heard by the multitudes.

Bilocation

Some have accomplished these first two abilities, even in recent times, but in Jeshua's time, he could multiply his Astral body many times as was necessary and simultaneously lower the vibration of all of his 'Astral duplicates' of himself at the same time, and by the way, speaking differently.

This 'magical' ability actually served two purposes: to reach more people far and wide and to provide for his protection against the Roman soldiers out looking to arrest him. The Romans would have their spies offering knowledge of where he would be, but they could never catch him because he was not physical and simply dissolved into thin air. A master of high spiritual ability could only do this feat. This ability he learned from Rishi and Lama masters while in India and Tibet.

Scriptural references in the cannon texts of the New Testament offer the first clue to this mystery. Joseph took Jeshua, at 12 years, with him to conduct business in Jerusalem. Jeshua left without telling Joseph of his intentions. When Joseph went to look for him, he found the boy inside the synagogue, addressing the priests on the deeper meanings of the scriptures from the Torah.

Following his astounding demonstration of knowledge of the Torah, even before his Bah Mitzvah, he disappeared. He did not reappear on the scene, according to the scriptures, until he was 30, the time he began his ministry.

The mainstream of Christian belief does not entertain what happened during those eighteen missing years. Certain esoteric scrolls of the Essene brotherhood recorded when they took him to India where he trained with Rishis and then to Tibet where he completed his training by the high Lamas to prepare for his mission to minister to the people of Jerusalem as the 'Mashiach' (Messiah).

The first requirement of the aspirant is to learn to control one's own vibratory frequency. This takes much effort and practice for years under the tutelage of a master. The author believes the first step for the layperson is to understand the need for whole brain synchrony and what is possible once accomplished. With a bifurcated (two hemispheres) brain, the mind, then it is compartmentalized and they can do nothing in this case.

Once the aspirant can raise their vibration of their consciousness to match the vibration of the Astral subtle body, mental traveling (remote viewing) becomes possible (this is called Clairvoyance by some). Then with the techniques made available within this text, one can enter the second phase and shift the Astral subtle body from the confines of the physical body and go to any place in the physical and to other dimensions in the spiritual realm, limited only to the skill to change the vibration at will.

Changing one's vibration is not limited to changing locations. This ability also offers the aspirant the ability to change the spacial distance of the atoms of the body, altering the actual distance in between, making the rarefication of density more dramatic, which can allow light normally reflected off the body to pass through the interstitial spaces making the individual become invisible. They usually leave this concept to a magician's 'slight of hand', meaning "now you see and now you don't." They spoke the true spiritual ability in the 'Aphorisms of Patanjuli,' regarding the attainment of yogic spiritual powers in the state of Samhadi, a deep state of concentration, contemplation and meditation. Changing the vibration of one's body relates to other 'gifts' such as levitation. Again, there are many instances where unique individuals presented this ability. One case on record is Saint Teresa of Avila who upon entering deep devotional prayer would suddenly go aloft several feet in the air above all the other nuns.

Epilogue

The focus is on the so called 'real' world. As many sages have said over many centuries from many sources of wisdom, 'the unseen world is far more important than what someone apparently can see with the physical sight.'

The author believes physicists seek sub-atomic particles and how they interact as a way of coming to an understanding of the 'real' world structure. Yet with their high-tech apparatus like particle accelerator/colliders in Europe, they keep finding more and more levels of finer particles, which they continue to name endlessly, while seeking the building blocks of matter.

A scientist by the name of Hanz Jenny, established an acoustical experimental laboratory to study sound visually to find the connection between sound and physical matter. He called this study Cymatics. The apparatus consisted of a Chladni plate (a metal plate suspended on a stand and the supporting stem had a magnetic coil wrapped around so that when electronic tones were applied the plate would vibrate accordingly. On the surface of the plate, he poured a fine powder.

Epilogue

The powder would gather where the sound was least and separate where the vibration was the strongest. The result was a perfect visual depiction of the sound. The Dr Jenny called in a Buddhist monk to utter the classic om mantra into a microphone. When the monk had finished the last of the intonation, the pattern on the plate was the Indian yantra of Om. This is the pattern of several interlocking triangles with a scalloped circle surrounding the triangles.

Their understanding is limited to physical structure. With these investigations, they do not come to an emotional understanding of the universe, meaning why and how did it come to pass, as an overriding 'Motus Operandi' behind the veil? Even with the field of advancing electronic technology, the components are shrinking to where the individual 'chips' are the size of atoms.

Technically, when they create these crystal wafers with billions of transistors embedded inside, it looks more like alchemy, and perhaps even magic. I believe it was said once by Arthur C. Clark, the inventor of the orbiting satellite, "they would describe Science to Aboriginal natives as pure magic."

Still, the cybernauts are unsatisfied with this level of technology. They want to pursue the quantum level of computing, which then depends on the sub-atomic particles shifting from wave structure to particle structure defining a fresh change of state; wave - particle and the transitional state. This idea suggests a new computer architecture that will be based on Quantum Mechanics. With this difference, it now borders on the unseen world more directly.

The cybernauts grow weary and doubt their ability to grasp this new frontier. They have begun the invention of artificial intelligence (AI), to assist them in navigating this brave new era of progress.

Raymond Kurzweil, a computer scientist, inventor and futurist, and Elon Musk with his 'Neurolink' project believe in a trans-humanistic world where AI chips implanted into the brain will function as mentor to the scientist/lay person alike. AI already exists in our world today; self-driving automobiles, home security systems with 'Alexa'

Epilogue

and our cell phones, to name a few. These are second level AI systems with limited sentience. The third level of AI (full sentient self-consciousness with self-directed behavior) would be required for this adaptation. Many scientists like Steven Hawking were very concerned. They announced that full sentient artificial intelligence would cease to be subservient and eventually become the dominant species to rule man or eliminate him altogether.

In terms of dreams versus 'reality' perception, the apparent difference that we are comparing is between dream/imagination and empirical reality, which makes up the 'real' world. Logically speaking, we are perceiving the real world in the same way we perceive the imaginary world of constructed digital reality.

We use the same neural networks to process and recognize the real world as with the digital world. If the virtual world is just as detailed sufficiently, so the mind cannot tell the difference anymore between the real and imaginary, how do we know that the so called 'real' world is real? Dreams are the same way.

So, who is to say with certainty that a dream is not real? Many spiritual teachers have proclaimed 'dreams can be real too.' Then perhaps we need to consider the aspect of the lucidity of dreams.

Since 2018, several scientists have stated publicly we are living in an artificial construct after they analyzed the mathematics of the 'real world' and discovered that the formulas describing a digital constructed world (the matrix) compared to the real are identical.

Many people believe that the imagination has no value. The reasoning comes from an ignorant upbringing. They teach us from childhood not to continue to admonish imagination beyond the sandbox! We quickly escorted children from the freedom of childhood to have imaginary friends, to 'buckle down' to the practical world of making a living, and to give up 'childish' dreams. We relegate dreams in this society to the artist and the visionary, but the average soul has to slug it out in the harsh reality that is their practical working environment.

Epilogue

Our imagination is a God given gift and separates us from the rest of the animal kingdom. A tiger or an elephant cannot imagine itself as something else, because they are aware but not self-aware. Only the human can do that. It is the underpinning of our ability to develop beyond our present state or condition, and our progress as a species depends on those brave souls that ignore their parent's advice.

In many spiritual teachings, a common concept presented: the valuable part of our being is not the crude matter of our mortal shell, but what is animating it. So the spiritual focus follows four basic approaches: the way of the Yogi (control of the mind); the way of the Monk (devotion and prayer); the way of the Fakir (controlling the mind by subjecting the body to extreme stress and pain); and finally the 'fourth way' which advocates the school of life itself and all the variety of random experience' is the only and best approach to connecting to the unseen reality.

Georges Gurjeiff taught in the early twentieth century. All distractions in life can remain as distractions or embraced and included in the focus necessary to glimpse the unseen.

According to many spiritual teachings, dreams are clearer by understanding the structure and function of the subtle nature of the human being.

The Chinese developed the concept of subtle neural pathways called 'acupuncture meridians' within the human body. These pathways conduct the 'life force' called 'Chi or Qui' that represents the powerhouse driving the body (the machine). There are central points where this energy collects and, by the East Indian philosophy, described as (chakras) visualized as lotus blossoms with increased numbers of petals from the coccyx to the crown.

In other spiritual systems, from older sources out of the fabled temples of Atlantis taught, these points called (Puukas) are really windows of perception defined by a series of specific vibrations of other dimensions of the soul, which intertwine with each other. The number of these points is seven. There also seems to be a rough correlation of these centers to the nerve plexuses

Epilogue

following up the spinal cord, from the coccyx to the crown, with rising complexity in their nerve ganglions.

The location of these centers begins at the base of the spine then rises to the next point just below the navel (Dan Tien), then next to the Solar Plexus, then the heart, throat, brow (between the eyes) and crown (at the top of the head). The last point sits just above the head, representing some cosmic connection to the quantum or 'heaven.' Some of these points correspond to spiritual or subtle bodies; the Astral; the Ethereal and the Causal. With dreams and their origins, the Astral body is key.

The Astral body vibrates very close to the physical body. It lives and functions within the physical body throughout the day, spiritually monitoring the comings and goings and mental and emotional attitudes and records that information in the spiritual 'book' of life called the 'Akashic record' about the individual soul. They keep this record as a reference for future soul incarnations.

At night, when the mind drops out of

consciousness, the Astral body vibration rises to the frequency of its natural habitat (Astral Kingdom) and then vacates the body to go to its normal residence there and deposits the daily record. The mind loses consciousness before this happens, but on certain occasions, the mind will remain awake and attempt to follow the Astral body towards its destination.

In that process, the mind may briefly encounter some aspects of the Astral kingdom before the separation occurs. The mind then may pick up on the information being deposited and try to reconstruct that data into a stream called a dream. These aspects may represent unresolved issues from the day which the mind perceives as loose ends and will construct the dream to make sense and or resolve the issues before it awakes for the next day.

Also, when the mind glimpses the Astral kingdom, it may also see events from the future and or the past because there is no time in the Astral world. So, everything is happening at once. Hence, the mind may perceive some part of that information as a future event. Thus, dreams can be prognostications or portents of things to come.

Dreams and accessing them can be an important tool for human evolution and development. Understanding the visual capacity in the act of imagination becomes helpful to spiritual understanding and soul development. We should not dismiss it as the idle fantasy of childish behavior. If you examine the action of a child at play; in one moment they are an astronaut and instantly in the next moment they can shift to being a cowboy or an Indian. In fact, this is the beginnings of imagination development and needs encouraging by adults.

Dreams can be a road map for the individual to monitor and track their own personal development. The importance of the use of imagination here is paramount, as well as exploring the Astral Kingdom, shifting from the physical to the nonphysical being, is the key to the future of human evolution.

The C.I.A. (Central Intelligence Agency) developed a program called (Project Stargate) during the cold war with Russia. This project was using the mind to seek impressions, using the intuitive imagination, about a distant or unseen subject, then provide that information (intel) about an object, event, person or location which is hidden from a physical view and separated at some distance. The research led by researchers Russell Targ and Harold Puthoff and later by Ingo Swann, Joseph McMoneagle and Courtney Brown psychically looking into the secret affaires of foreign governments by using this technique called (Remote Viewing).

There was only one who showed this ability with incredible accuracy, and that was Ingo Swann. With more advanced technology to view distant places remotely, such as drones, the use of remote viewing waned.

There are hundreds of books written about the paranormal and psychic phenomenon. The various works represent a vast perspective of these phenomenon and still there is an undercurrent by many that there is a fundamental disbelief in all this, even with scientific evidence. Dr. J. B. Rhine

Epilogue

at Duke university conducted double blind studies of students to determine if there was evidence of psychic ability beyond the realm of chance.

This was done with a series of character cards presented without showing the subject the characters. Dr. Rhine also created faraday cages (two boxed rooms lined with copper mesh to block all electromagnetic influences. Subjects were placed inside each shielded room then ideas and images presented to one subject would then be telepathically transmitted to the other. In certain cases transmission was successful. This proved that the mental energy used during telepathic contact had nothing to do with electromagnetics.

Bibliography

Biblical References:

The term is derived from Ecclesiastes 12:6-7 in the Jewish Bible or Christian Old Testament.

As translated from the original Hebrew in The Complete Tanakh:[6]

"Before the silver cord snaps, and the golden fountain is shattered, and the pitcher breaks at the fountain, and the wheel falls shattered into the pit. And the dust returns to the earth as it was, and the spirit returns to God, Who gave it."

As rendered in the Authorised Version:

"Or ever the silver cord be loosed, or the golden bowl be broken, or the pitcher be broken at the fountain, or the wheel broken at the cistern. Then shall the dust return to the earth as it was: and the spirit shall return unto God who gave it."

Or from the New International Version:

"Remember him—before the silver cord is severed, or the golden bowl is broken; before the pitcher is shattered at the spring, or the wheel broken at the well, and the dust returns to the ground it came from, and the spirit returns to God who gave it."

These verses, Ecclesiastes 12:6-7, are variously translated, and there is a lack of consensus among Bible commentators as to its meaning. Matthew Henry's commentary, for example, states that the silver cord refers simply to the "spinal marrow."

References:

1. Bailey, Alice. Education in the New Age (PDF). Lucis Trust. pp. 19, 21, 76–9. ISBN 9780853301059.
2. Jump up to: a b c Smed, Jouni A. (2013). "Out-of-body experience studies". www.monroeinstitute.org. The Monroe Institute. Archived from the original on 2013-04-15.
3. Jump up to: a b Ballabene, Alfred (1997). "The silver cord (observations and traditions)".
4. Jump up to: a b Blackmore, Susan (2004). "Out-of-body experience". In Gregory, Richard L. (ed.). The Oxford Companion to the Mind (2nd ed.). Oxford University Press. ISBN 9780198662242.
5. "Life after death". hpb.theosophy.org.nz. Auckland Theosophical Centre: HPB Lodge. 2013-06-08.

6. "The Complete Tanach with Rashi's Commentary - English translation with Rashi's commentary".

7. Henry, Matthew; Scott, Thomas (1835). A Commentary Upon the Holy Bible. Vol. 3: Job to Salomon's song. London: Religious Tract Society. p. 496.

Fredrick, James; Tildes, Olga (1946). The Silver Cord or Life Here and Hereafter. Christopher Pub.

Barham, Martha; Greene, James Tom (1986). The Silver Cord: Lifeline to the Unobstructed. De Vorss & Co.

1. Lack, Caleb (April 2020). "Depression: Is Psychoanalytic dream interpretation useful?". Skeptical Inquirer. 44 (2): 51.

2. Domhoff, G. William. "Moving dream theory beyond Freud and Jung". Dreamresearch.net. University of California Santa Cruz: dreamresearch.net. Retrieved 25 March 2020.

3. Domhoff, G. William (2000). "The misinterpretation of dreams". American Scientist. 88 (2): 175–178.

4. Jump up to: a b c d Morewedge, Carey K.; Norton, Michael I. (2009). "When dreaming is believing: The (motivated) interpretation of dreams". Journal of Personality and Social Psychology. 96(2): 249–264. doi:10.1037/a0013264. PMID 19159131.

5. Jump up to: a b c d e f g h i j k l m n o p Black, Jeremy; Green, Anthony (1992). Gods, Demons and Symbols of Ancient Mesopotamia: An Illustrated Dictionary. Austin, Texas: University of Texas Press. pp. 71–72, 89–90. ISBN 0714117056.

6. Jump up to: a b Seligman, K. (1948), Magic, Supernaturalism and Religion. New York: Random House

7. Jump up to: a b Oppenheim, L.A. (1966). Mantic Dreams in the Ancient Near East in G. E. Von Grunebaum & R. Caillois (Eds.), The Dream and Human Societies (pp. 341–350). London, England: Cambridge University Press.

8. Thompson, R. (1930) The Epic of Gilgamesh. Oxford: Oxford University Press.

9. George, A. trans. (2003) The Babylonian Gilgamesh Epic: Critical Edition and Cuneiform

Texts. Oxford, UK: Oxford University Press.
10. Oppenheim, A. (1956) The interpretation of dreams in the ancient Near East with a translation of an Assyrian dreambook. Transactions of the American Philosophical Society, 46(3): 179–373. p. 247.
11. Jump up to: a b Caillois, R. (1966). Logical and Philosophical Problems of the Dream. In G.E. Von Grunebaum & R. Caillos (Eds.), The Dream and Human Societies(pp. 23–52). London, England: Cambridge University Press.
12. Nils P. Heessel : Divinatorische Texte I : ... oneiromantische Omina. Harrassowitz Verlag, 2007.
13. Artemidorus (1990) The Interpretation of Dreams: Oneirocritica. White, R., trans., Torrance, CA: Original Books, 2nd Edition.
14. Jump up to: a b Freud, S. (1900) The Interpretation of Dreams. New York: Avon, 1980.
15. (Haque 2004, p. 376)
16. (Haque 2004, p. 375)
17. (Haque 2004, p. 361)
18. (Haque 2004, p. 363)

19. Lutz, Peter L. (2002), The Rise of Experimental Biology: An Illustrated History,
Humana Press, p. 60, ISBN 0-89603-835-1
20. Ibn Khaldun, Franz Rosenthal, N.J. Dawood (1967), The Muqaddimah, trans., p. 338, Princeton University Press, ISBN 0-691-01754-9
21. Lofty Principles of Dream Interpretation, "Inner Chapters 1–4"
22. Lofty Principles of Dream Interpretation, "Inner Chapter 5"
23. Lofty Principles of Dream Interpretation, "Inner Chapters 6–9"
24. Lofty Principles of Dream Interpretation, "Inner Chapter 10"
25. Johnson, M.; Kahan, T.; Raye, C. (1984). "Dreams and reality monitoring". Journal of Experimental Psychology: General. 113 (3): 329–344. doi:10.1037/0096-3445.113.3.329. PMID 6237167.
26. Blechner, M (2005). "Elusive illusions: Reality judgment and reality assignment in dreams and waking life". Neuro-Psychoanalysis. 7: 95–101. doi:10.1080/15294145.2005.10773477. S2CID

145533839.
27. Nagera, Humberto, ed. (2014) [1969]. "Manifest content (pp. 52ff.)". Basic Psychoanalytic Concepts on the Theory of Dreams. Abingdon-on-Thames: Routledge. ISBN 978-1-31767047-6.
28. Nagera, Humberto, ed. (2014) [1969]. "Latent dream-content (pp. 31ff.)". Basic Psychoanalytic Concepts on the Theory of Dreams. Abingdon-on-Thames: Routledge. ISBN 978-1-31767048-3.
29. Freud, Sigmund, 1856-1939. (2010). The interpretation of dreams. Strachey, James. New York: Basic Books A Member of the Perseus Books Group. ISBN 9780465019779. OCLC 434126117.
30. Matalon, Nadav (2011). "The Riddle Of Dreams". Philosophical Psychology. 24 (4): 517–536. doi:10.1080/09515089.2011.556605. S2CID 144246389.
31. Wilson, Cynthia (3 April 2012). "Remembering and Understanding your Dreams". Womenio. Retrieved 28 May2012.
32. Gray, R. (9 January 2012). "Lecture Notes: Freud's Conception of the Psyche (Unconscious)

and His Theory of Dreams". University of Washington. Retrieved 28 May2012.

33. Freud, S. (1900) op.cit., (1919 edition), p. 397

34. Jung, C.G. (1902) The associations of normal subjects. In: Collected Works of C. G. Jung, vol. 2. Princeton, NJ: Princeton University Press, pp. 3–99.

35. Jacobi, J. (1973) The Psychology of C. G. Jung. New Haven, CT: Yale University Press.

36. Jump up to: a b Storr, Anthony (1983). The Essential Jung. New York. ISBN 0-691-02455-3.

37. Lone, Zauraiz (2018-09-26). "Jung's Dream Theory and Modern Neuroscience: From Fallacies to Facts". World of Psychology. Retrieved 2019-04-30.

38. Jung, C.G. (1948) General aspects of dream psychology. In: Dreams. trans., R. Hull. Princeton, NJ: Princeton University Press, 1974, pp. 23–66.

39. Jump up to: a b Doyle, D. John (2018). What does it mean to be human? Life, Death, Personhood and the Transhumanist Movement. Cham, Switzerland: Springer. p. 173. ISBN 9783319949505. OCLC 1050448349.

40. Jung, C.G. (1948) op.cit.
41. Stekel, W. (1911) Die Sprache des Traumes (The Language of the Dream).
Wiesbaden: J.F. Berman
42. Sullivan, H.S. (1953) The Interpersonal Theory of Psychiatry. New York: Norton.
43. Jung, Carl (1934). The Practice of Psychotherapy. The Practical Use of Dream-analysis. p. 147. ISBN 0-7100-1645-X.
44. Calvin S. Hall. "A Cognitive Theory of Dreams". dreamresearch.net. Retrieved 7 October 2010.
45. Faraday, Ann. The Dream Game. p. 3.
46. Clift, Jean Dalby; Clift, Wallace (1984). Symbols of Transformation in Dreams. The Crossroad Publishing Company.
ISBN 0-8245-0653-7.; Clift, Jean Dalby; Clift, Wallace (1988). The Hero Journey in Dreams. The Crossroad Publishing Company.
ISBN 0-8245-0889-0.; Clift, Jean Dalby (1992). Core Images of the Self: A Symbolic Approach to Healing and Wholeness. The Crossroad Publishing Company. ISBN 0-8245-1218-9.

www.ingramcontent.com/pod-product-compliance
Lightning Source LLC
Chambersburg PA
CBHW061728070526
44583CB00024B/3057